THE NEXTGEN GUIDE TO CAR COLLECTING

Inspiring | Educating | Creating | Entertaining

Brimming with creative inspiration, how-to projects, and useful information to enrich your everyday life, quarto.com is a favorite destination for those pursuing their interests and passions.

First Published in 2022 by Motorbooks, an imprint of The Quarto Group,
100 Cummings Center, Suite 265-D, Beverly, MA 01915, USA.
T (978) 282-9590 F (978) 283-2742 Quarto.com

Motorbooks titles are also available at discount for retail, wholesale, promotional, and bulk purchase. For details, contact the Special Sales Manager by email at specialsales@quarto.com or by mail at The Quarto Group, Attn: Special Sales Manager, 100 Cummings Center, Suite 265-D, Beverly, MA 01915, USA.

26 25 24 23 22   1 2 3 4 5

ISBN: 978-0-7603-7337-8

Digital edition published in 2022
eISBN: 978-0-7603-7338-5

Library of Congress Control Number: 2022934539

Design and layout: Burge Agency

Printed in China

THE NEXTGEN GUIDE TO CAR COLLECTING

HOW TO BUY, SELL, LIVE WITH, AND LOVE A COLLECTIBLE CAR

ROBERT C. YEAGER
INTRODUCTION BY MCKEEL HAGERTY

motorbooks

CONTENTS

"FOR FUTURE CAR GUYS
CALVIN AND CASPER
MEIERS: MAY THE ROAD
AHEAD BE SMOOTH
AND THE TWISTIES
ALWAYS FUN."

ACKNOWLEDGMENTS

The author extends his thanks and appreciation to those whose help and contributions made this book possible. These include (but are not limited to) McKeel Hagerty, who provided the book's introduction and gave the project its critical initial support; Hagerty's Brian Rabold, vice president of Automotive Intelligence; John Wiley, the firm's manager of Analytics; and Andy Heller, its director of Executive Communications. The author is especially grateful to Kandace Hawkinson and Sandra Button, senior editor and chairman, respectively, of the Pebble Beach Concours d'Elegance, who have supported, encouraged, and assisted him throughout his automotive writing career. And thanks too to Al McEwan—who with his wife Sandi organizes and directs the annual Pebble Beach Motoring Classic—for many last-minute fact checks.

Among those contributing notable content and information: Jonathan Gill, of mpacreative. com in Weybridge, Surrey, and especially David Burgess-Wise for sharing often harrowing firsthand archives of the London-Brighton Run; auto writer and former General Motors quality manager Jack Keebler; Jim Fasnacht, Ruxton authority nonpareil; Kevin Cahill of the W. Edwards Deming Institute and Bill Scherkenbach, the late Dr. Deming's globe-trotting assistant; extraordinary female activist-enthusiasts Tabetha Hammer, Caroline Cassini, Theresa Gilpatrick, Cindy Sisson, and Laura Foster; Amanda Gutierrez and Christopher Paulsen from McPherson College in McPherson, Kansas; Winthrop Baum, president of the Mercedes Benz Club of America's Westchester-Connecticut Section; Mark Hyman, founder and president of Hyman Ltd. in St. Louis, Missouri; and Randy Nonnenberg, founder and president of Bring-a-Trailer, whose thoughtful insights helped inform several pieces for the *New York Times* as well as this book. Thanks also to Luca Malin, of Malin Communication in Rovigo, Italy, for translation help and assistance in obtaining *Indomita*, his biography of the remarkable Baroness Maria Antonietta Avanzo.

For freely sharing their knowledge and passion: car buddies, friends, collectors, enthusiasts, and helpers Hank Johnson, Kurt Glaubitz, Ed Adams, Dan Vierra, Michael Boloyan, and Remo Biaggi. Recognition must also include members of Berkeley, California's unique and globally influential vintage car community: Bruce and Spencer Trenery, Patrick and Tazio Ottis, and Glenn Oliveria. Thanks also to James Cobb, legendary Automobiles editor of the *New York Times*, and Norman Mayersohn, his equally expert assistant, plus current *Times* editors Randy Pennell and Justin Swanson—singularly and together, they helped a journalist write about a subject he loves for the world's greatest newspaper. Thanks also go to Terry Dunkle, the author's longtime originals editor at *Reader's Digest*, who taught him many tricks of the writing trade; and, of course, to his ultimate editor in chief and first reader, Judith Ann Yeager.

Robert C. Yeager, The Sea Ranch, California

INTRODUCTION
By McKeel Hagerty

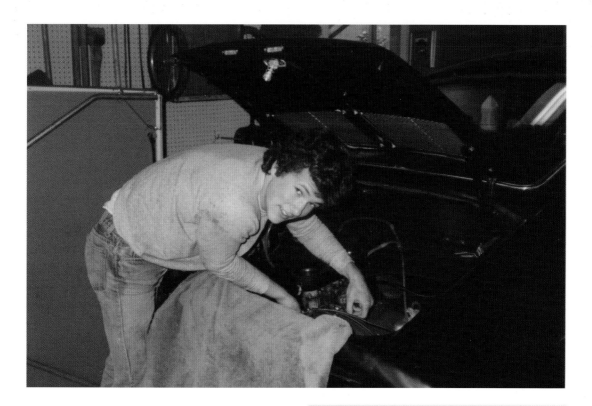

"To be human is to collect things. We've always done so. Some people collect coins. Some collect comic books. Some collect tea kettles, stamps, sneakers, or first-edition Beatles albums on vinyl."

Bringing her back to life, a wrench at a time.

I happen to collect cars and driving experiences. I don't know why, exactly. My dad, an insurance man by trade, was a shade-tree mechanic in his spare time, and we kids knew that if we wanted to spend time with him it would be under the hood of a car, passing him a wrench. And while that certainly lit the fire in me, who can really say why an interest becomes a passion and a passion becomes a lifelong god-I-love-this obsession?

Perhaps it doesn't matter. The truth is that human beings collect what we collect for a million different reasons—status, self-expression, to share a passion and be part of a group or community. And the point of any pastime or hobby is simply whether it makes you feel good and brings you joy.

Cars meet that test for me. And if you're reading this book, I'm guessing they do for you as well.

So, welcome! Consider this book your on-ramp to the world of car collecting. We are definitely not alone in our proclivity. America, after all, is a car-crazy country and has been for more than a century. Nothing much has changed. Today, in fact, it is estimated that approximately *69 million* Americans would describe themselves as full-fledged "automotive enthusiasts," which I take to mean people who get that tickle of excitement just thinking about their next car, their next drive, or their next wrench session. (My joke when people ask me what my favorite car is after a lifetime of collecting is "My next one.")

Sixty-nine million is a big number. But this pastime of ours is far bigger than that, I suspect. That figure, for instance, doesn't include the far greater number of people who would consider themselves, to coin a phrase, "car curious." In other words, people who have always liked cars beyond their utilitarian function—as a means to get from point A to point B—but don't yet own a classic, vintage, or "just for fun" collectible vehicle, whether it's a car, truck, or motorcycle.

Whatever your experience in the car world, I can assure you that you are in for a treat. Bob Yeager, your author, whom I've known for years, is one of the finest automotive journalists and storytellers in the land, and in his more-than-capable hands you will learn just about everything there is to know about finding, buying, selling, investing in, and loving a collectible car.

A generational project gets father and son care.

Before we let Bob get on with it, though, a quick thought about the term *collectible*. It's only a word, just like the terms *classic cars* or *vintage cars*. There are a lot of myths about the collectible car world, and the biggest is that it's a hobby for the wealthy, the old, or those stuck in the 1950s. It's not. It's for everyone, no matter their taste. It's for the young and the old. The wealthy, and not so wealthy. It's for speed freaks, Sunday cruisers, and low-riders. Pickup lovers. Tinkerers. People who like ripping it up on a track. People who jones for '70s, '80s, '90s, or even post-millennium cars. It's for people who like old station wagons with faux wood-grain panels and a rear-facing back seat. It's for people who like modern muscle. (We are in the Golden Age of Muscle at the moment, in my opinion.) The definition of a collectible car is simply this: a car, truck, SUV, pickup, or motorcycle that you like. That's it. That's all.

In my mind, all cars are worthy, regardless of their book worth. Hagerty, my company, operates numerous Concours d'Elegance events across the nation that showcase the best of the best. And I love those cars. They're wonderful to look at, and even more fun to drive if you get the chance. Hagerty insures a lot of those best-of-the-best cars, but we also insure many more cars that all of us recognize and have driven. Here, for instance, are the top ten vehicles that we insure: Corvettes, Mustangs, Chevy C10 ½-ton pickups, Camaros, Chevrolet Bel Airs, Model As, Beetles, Thunderbirds, F-100 ½-ton trucks, and Impalas.

Some of those vehicles are now iconic. Some are extremely valuable, depending on the year and condition. And, yes, some are bought because they are wonderful investments. But the vast majority are bought simply because they ignite something in the soul of the people who bought them.

The longer you're around the hobby, the more you'll notice that's what it's all about—cool cars, cool roads, and shared experiences with people who share the fascination. What's cool is defined by the owner. Some people want a car just like the one their parents or grandparents owned. Others love convertibles or hot rods. (Deuces, I will admit, are very, very cool.) Some crave a Model A or Model T. Some want a car just like the one they saw in a movie. (I've always been a James Bond fan, so an Aston Martin will grab my attention any time.)

There's no right, wrong, or better in the car world. There are just cars and the people who love them. Did you know, for instance, that one of the fastest growing segments of the enthusiast vehicle market today is pickups and SUVs, especially old Broncos? Who would have thought!

Cars built in Japan are hot, too. The Mazda Miata, in particular, has become the signature car in the recent evolution of the car world. People cruise them, race them, modify them. There was a great *New York Times* article about Miata love that said: "Owners tend to drive their Miatas, rather than merely admire them as garage ornaments. Mr. Hembrough put 19,000 miles on his over three years of ownership. To relax, Sam Abuelsamid, principal analyst for e-mobility at Guidehouse Insights in Detroit, regularly takes out his 1990 Miata—a very early model built in October 1989. 'My dog, Rosie, likes riding in it,' Mr. Abuelsamid said. 'She's tall enough to stick her head out.'"

That's wonderful. The truth about the hobby is this: A vast variety of cars and trucks have been produced over the decades, and people love them for an equally vast number of reasons. I've seen countless expressions of that fact, but here's my favorite. One summer a few years

ago, I was out driving the vineyard-strewn roads that crisscross the lovely peninsula where I live. And what to my wandering eyes did appear but a touring group of people all driving . . . Pontiac Azteks, the much maligned midsize crossover SUV that kind of looks like a basketball shoe on wheels. They obviously didn't care what the

A lifetime keeper, fully restored in Original Polo Red.

critics think. They were having a grand old time. It made me happy the whole day.

That's the car hobby writ small. You love what you love for the reasons you love it.

All that matters is that you enjoy the ride. I'll see you out there.

Below:
SUTTON HOO "THE DIG"
Considered among the most
significant medieval burial sites
ever discovered in Europe. Inside
the mound lay the decayed skeleton
of a funeral ship for an Anglo-Saxon
warrior king. Its story retold in
the 2021 Netflix film *The Dig*, the
1939 discovery by self-trained
archeologist Basil Brown included
elegant feasting vessels, silverware
from Byzantium, and handcrafted
gold buckles and adornments. The
Sutton Hoo site derives its name
from old English and is located in
Suffolk County, England.

PREFACE

"The past speaks." So states Basil Brown, self-schooled archeologist, in the British film *The Dig*. Later, the movie builds on his remark.

"You've always said your work isn't about the past or even the present," says his wife. *"It's for the future, so that the next generations can know where they came from. The line that joins them to their forebears."*

Mrs. Pretty, owner of the Suffolk County property where Mr. Brown wields his picks and shovels, puts it even more succinctly: "From the first human handprint on a cave wall," she says, "we are part of something continuous. So we don't really die."

Does a similar thirst for our links to the past explain why we cherish classic automobiles? Do the visibly worn original leather seats—surely touched by the actor's very own fingers—tell us why Gary Cooper's 1935 SSJ Duesenberg became the highest priced American automobile ever sold at public auction?* Do such signs of humanity, as Mrs. Pretty suggests,

GARY COOPER DUESY
Actor Gary Cooper's 1935 SSJ convertible—one of only two made—became the most expensive American car ever publicly sold when it crossed the block for $22 million at Gooding & Co.'s Pebble Beach auction in 2018. Part of a studio promotion, Cooper paid only $5,000 for the car when new. Considered by some to be America's first "supercar," the Duesy's supercharged straight-eight boasted 400 horsepower and could reach a top speed of 140 miles per hour.

confirm the connectedness of our past, present, and future—even, perhaps, a universal yearning for eternal life? Could all of the above be true? Indeed, your author passionately believes it is as important to preserve, protect, and enjoy these artifacts of automotive history as it is to revere the buried remains of a funeral ship for a sixth-century Anglo-Saxon king.

In the end, like the diggings in the chalky soil on Mrs. Pretty's estate and the cracked leather seats in Gary Cooper's old roadster, classic automobiles call out important moments in our

---

*Sold for $22 million at Gooding & Co. auction at Pebble Beach, CA, in 2018.

PHIL LINHARES & HIS 'BIRTHDAY' MGTC
A retired museum curator, Phil Linhares first spotted an MG TC in the window of a Tucker dealership as a boy in Modesto, California. He purchased this car in 2021 after discovering it was built in 1948 on his birthday. Manufactured from 1945 to 1949, the TC was an updated model of the 1930s MG Midget. The TC's postwar sales far exceeded MG's expectations, many being purchased by returning U.S. servicemen.

lives, often experienced in youth. This writer recalls the first time, as a gawking teenager, he laid eyes on an Italian car at a dealership in Beverly Hills, California. Is it surprising that his initial purchase of a vintage automobile would be a 1959 Alfa Romeo Giulietta Spider? McKeel Hagerty, who wrote this book's introduction, dug his first collectible, a 1967 Porsche 911S, out

of a Michigan snowbank when he was thirteen. He then spent several years restoring the vehicle with his father; he still owns and drives it to this day.

Kurt Glaubitz, a Gen Xer from Mill Valley, California, bought his 1992 Land Rover Defender as a project he could do with his teenage son, Cole, ignoring—or learning to love—its scrawny-necked snorkel (for fording rivers) and its boxy lines. As a teenager, Mr. Glaubitz had restored a Rover sedan with his father. "My favorite memories of my dad are working beside him under the bonnet of that car," he recalls.

Phil Linhares, now in his eighties, remembers the first time he saw an MG TC. "I was ten, living in Modesto," said the retired Oakland, California, museum curator. "It was bright red, sitting in the Tucker dealer's showroom. I thought it was the most beautiful car I'd ever seen."

Seventy-one years later, the still-youthful-appearing Mr. Linhares spotted an online ad for a cream-colored 1949 MG TC with olive green cycle fenders. His pulse quickened when he read the car's original "build sheet." Its English maker had completed the roadster exactly seven decades and one year before his own birthday on August 8. He bought the MG on the spot.

Despite the continuing importance of veteran collectors such as Mr. Linhares, however, *How to Buy, Sell, Live with, and Love a Collectible Car* is, as its cover suggests, a guidebook aimed at a new generation. Using proprietary insurance policy data, Hagerty examined more than 18,000 transactions from 2016 to 2018 in which vintage cars changed hands from older to younger buyers. The firm found the largest single group, or 22 percent of all purchasers, were Gen Xers like Mr. Glaubitz—that is, buyers aged roughly from their late thirties to their early fifties, at that time.

Those findings were affirmed by Michael Caimano, who specializes in vintage car sales for Bonham's auction house. "Close to half our sales are to that (age) group," he told the *New York Times* in June 2019. "They've achieved a place in life that's put them in the prime collection-building years." At the same time, Mr. Caimano noted, millennials were "beginning to stick their toes in the water, particularly with collectibles in the $50,000 to $200,000 range."

Despite the fact that buyers born during the post–World War II "baby boom" still dominate the purchase of million-dollar-and-up cars, said Hagerty, "2018 will be remembered as the year that younger car lovers took the wheel from older generations." For the immediate future, most of those car lovers will likely be the Gen Xers described by Mr. Caimano. But within five years, Hagerty predicts, millennials will become the hobby's single largest group of buyers. Indeed, well-heeled millennials currently make up the second largest group after baby boomers who seek the firm's insurance data on $10 million–plus cars.

"What we're really seeing is a progression in our hobby," said Terry McGean, editor in chief of *Hemmings Motor News* in comments to the *New York Times*. "It's a new group of people interested in a new generation of cars."

Those newly desirable autos include specimens most serious collectors wouldn't have sniffed at a few years ago—including '90s models like Mr. Glaubitz's Defender and Japanese cars like Toyota's Supra and Honda's NSX.

With apologies to Gary Cooper's Duesenberg, the notion that a collectible car must be hand built in low volume no longer carries the cachet it once did. "The younger generation doesn't even think about cars being handmade anymore," said Mr. McGean. Similarly, the word *vintage* no longer means what it once did. Low-mileage 1990s Toyota Supras and late-model American muscle cars routinely command high five figures, and sometimes six; when new, many of these cars sold for $30,000 to $40,000, some for far less.

Thus, although it includes an overview of 1930s, '40s, '50s, and '60s European and American classics, *NextGen Guide* focuses on cars built during and after the 1970s. Separate chapters highlight American, European, and Japanese cars and especially those models that show up in the rankings of Hagerty's most accessed valuation tools. Also noted: Bring-a-Trailer.com's Top Ten Surprising Results (which previously included such shockers as a 1985 Mercedes 300 Turbo Diesel that went for $44,000; a '91 GMC Syclone that made $50K; and a tiny Austin "Beach Car" with no windows, 10-inch wheels, and a petite motorcycle-size engine, that drew a final bid of more than $230,000.)

AUSTIN MINI 'BEACH CAR'
One of only 14 Austin Mini "Beach Cars," this vehicle was a promotional gift to American dealers by the British Motor Company during the 1960s. Owned for 57 years by San Francisco's Mary Falvey, whose father had been a prominent European car distributor in Michigan, the Lilliputian vehicle sold after spirited bidding for $230,000 at a Bring-a-Trailer auction in 2020.

In "Buying Your First Collectible Car Successfully", we coach readers on how to make such a purchase without suffering "buyer's remorse." Along the way, *NextGen Guide* identifies five critical keys to a happy vintage vehicle/owner marriage: 1) possessing sufficient discretionary cash for the initial purchase; 2) conducting "deep-dive curation," i.e., intense prepurchase research into a given model's known strengths and shortcomings; 3) obtaining the complete history of a vehicle's ownership; 4) securing a competent prepurchase inspection (PPI) of a given vehicle's current condition before buying and a proficient local mechanic thereafter; and 5) having adequate garage or storage space.

Another chapter suggests why the popularity of pre- and even early post–2000 cars may be destined to grow (think intrusive electronic bric-a-brac, annoying warning devices, occasionally dangerous automation, and the still-large number of consumers for whom "self-driving" means driving themselves). None of this dictates that our chosen models need forego such amenities as power disc brakes and steering, or even automatic transmissions and air-conditioning. Indeed, some of the cars we love most include those niceties and more. What our ideal buyer will not find, however, are blinking touch screens, buzzing side sensors, and autopilot features. Our cars demand that drivers drive.

A separate chapter, "NextGen Women Love Cars Too," reports on the growing presence of women among vintage car enthusiasts. Another chapter discusses the significant increases in quality and reliability of post-1970s machines. It describes the important role philosopher-engineer W. Edwards Deming played in influencing the manufacturing processes of Japanese and eventually European and American automakers. Finally, the book will tell readers why expectations that collectible cars can survive the coming onslaught of EV Power may not be far fetched. Indeed, a host of recent developments could actually extend the lives of collectible automobiles, especially as more urban dwellers opt for alternate means of everyday transport. Among them: ride-hailing and -sharing services, expanded public transit, even rental bikes and scooters. So-called "garage condos," classic car country clubs, and other urban-rural fringe developments also add flexibility to the use and life spans of older cars.

Also described are how the internet and social media have changed the collector car experience and marketplace. The *NextGen Guide* explicitly recognizes this trend in chapter 8, "Buying Your First Classic Car *Successfully.*" Besides making a wider variety of cars available

GLAUBITZ AND SON
Kurt Glaubitz and his son Cole huddle under the hood of their vintage Land Rover Defender. Labeled "the coolest SUV around" in being named to Hagerty's Bull Market List for 2022, Mr. Glaubitz's boxy 1992 model came equipped with a snorkel (for fording rivers) and cost $18,000 in 2019. Hagerty put the vehicle's current value in excellent condition ranging between $61,000–$77,000.

to new buyers, the internet has helped introduce a new era of honesty and integrity to the process. Nothing, however, can replace getting behind the wheel of an actual car. Armed with marque-specific knowledge and preparation, a novice can successfully navigate the internet and take full advantage of what it has to offer, namely, a golden age of buying, selling, and enjoying vintage automobiles. Of course, the question today remains much what it was in 1958, when Floyd Clymer published *Buy an Antique Car*—namely, how do you purchase a used automobile you don't know much about? It is this question our book seeks to answer.

1993 TOYOTA SUPRA
"Japanese cars are getting to be full-fledged collectibles," proclaimed the *New York Times* in 2019. Especially favored by NextGen collectors, Toyota's venerable Supra cars rank at the front of the pack. Starting as a version of the Celica hatchback in 1979, Supra went on to become a force in its own right, winning *Motor Trend's* Import Car of the Year award and its repeated inclusion on *Car and Driver's* 10 Best Lists in the early 1980s. The 5th Generation Supra was unveiled in 2019.

THE WORLD'S OLDEST MOTORING EVENT
The London to Brighton run began in 1896 to celebrate "emancipation" from Britain's onerous 4-miles-per-hour "red-flag" speed limit. The car below, a 1901 De Dion Bouton with bodywork by H.J. Mulliner, has been a regular on the run since 1936. Here seen crossing Westminster Bridge in the 1970s, the car was affectionately called "Martha" by Col. H.J. Wellingham, one of its previous owners.

1

AUTOMOTIVE ORIGINS

From the days of brass headlamps, hand cranks, and "motoring dusters," cars have fascinated humankind.

"Owners and drivers should remember that motor cars are on trial in England and that any rashness or carelessness might injure the industry in this country."

Instructions to first participants in
London-Brighton race

With this somber warning, the London to Brighton "Emancipation Run" began on a rainy Saturday, November 14, 1896. It was a time of widespread fear and distrust of motorized transport. Indeed, in America, a proposed law would have required horseless carriage operators encountering livestock to immediately stop, dismantle their vehicle, *and conceal its parts* until the beastly pedestrians were "sufficiently pacified." England's "Emancipation Run" was actually a celebration of the repeal of that nation's onerous "Red Flag Act." In addition to its 4-mile-per-hour speed limit on country roads (2-miles-per-hour limit in town), the widely loathed measure required that *any* "self-propelled" vehicle be preceded by a person walking at least 60 yards ahead and carrying a red flag. Not surprisingly, onlookers cheered when—at a breakfast preceding the run—Tory politician Lord Winchelsea ripped a symbolic red flag in half.

That event, soon to be known as the "London to Brighton Veteran Car Run," launched a new era in our fascination with the automobile. The 54-mile trip, whose participating cars must have been

1915 FORD MODEL T
Called the Model T because it followed the Model S (the Model A was introduced in 1903), Ford eventually built 15 million T's between 1908 and 1927, the longest production run of any automobile until it was surpassed by the Volkswagen Beetle in 1972. A new model T cost some $825 in 1915; today collectible T's sell for $15,000–$20,000, depending on model and condition.

1886 BENZ PATENT MOTORWAGEN
Widely considered the world's first practical automobile, the petrol-powered Motorwagen cost 600 German marks upon introduction, or about $150 in then-current U.S. dollars. The car competed in rallies until the 1950s according to Mercedes-Benz. An unrestored 1888 model is believed to the oldest automobile in original condition.

built before 1905, has been held—with breaks for World War II, gas rationing in 1947, and the 2020s COVID pandemic—every year since its revival in 1927. Today it stands as the world's longest-running motoring event and by far the largest gathering of antique cars. As they did in the beginning, drivers and passengers don leather "dusters," headgear, and goggles and brace themselves for chilly temperatures and a wet, bouncy ride on England's A23 highway. In the beginning, only seventeen of the original thirty-three cars went the distance; today, about 90 percent sputter all the way to Brighton's Preston Park. To dispel any notion of the run as a race, order of finish is not recorded; however, the lucky few who arrive by 4:30 p.m. receive a medal. Celebrities and notables frequently participate; in 1971, Queen Elizabeth II rode as a passenger in a 1900 Daimler originally owned by her great-grandfather, King Edward VII. On a typical run, as many as a half million spectators line the roadway.

In important ways, such occasions fueled enthusiasm for the automobile and, subsequently, the showing of cars and car collecting. In fact, the day before the first London to Brighton run, participants assembled to display their vehicles to the public. Large crowds gathered. "Most Londoners had never seen a car before," wrote Richard Abatto in *Concours Retrospective*, "and the roar of the engines, the smell of the gasoline, and the appearance of the new contraptions caused great astonishment among a group of people accustomed to horse-drawn carriages."

Twelve years later, when Henry Ford introduced the Model T, the world changed forever. Initially priced at $825, the little black car would cost only $380 when final models rolled off the assembly line in 1927, an economic miracle made possible by mass production and integrated components. Between those years, the T's tire print would spread across the globe, from Amazonian rubber forests to satellite manufacturing plants in Ireland, New Zealand, Canada, and beyond. In less than a decade, the Model T would account for 50 percent of all the cars on the planet.

It had taken a long time to get there. Although Karl Benz designed, built, and patented the world's first production automobile (the "motorwagen") in 1886, efforts to develop independent mobilized transport had begun centuries before.

"Open top three-wheeler. Italian design and craftsmanship. Zero mpg, no emissions. Easy parking and programmable steering."

This 2004 mock advertisement in The Guardian heralded the development of the world's first self-propelled vehicle, designed by none other than Leonardo da Vinci in or around 1487. Through the intervening years, efforts to build the car failed due to its notoriously secretive inventor's unclear sketches. In 2004, however, a team at Italy's Institute and Museum of the History of Science used computer-aided design to build a one-third scale model based on da Vinci's drawings. They discovered the car's power came from coiled springs housed in cylinders inside its frame. The vehicle worked much like a child's wind-up toy by rotating the wheels backward—that is, opposite their intended direction. According to The Guardian's John Hooper, in a 2004 article, da Vinci scholars had long suspected that the seatless car had been intended as an attraction at Renaissance festivals. "It has a brake," Hooper wrote, "that can be released at a distance by an operator with a hidden rope, making it appear to start by itself."

In 1672, Jesuit missionary Ferdinand Verbiest made a small, steam-powered vehicle for the

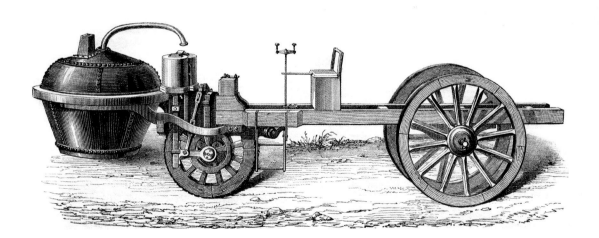

CUGNOT STEAM CAR
More than a century before the Motorwagen, French inventor and army Captain Nicholas Joseph Cugnot designed the first self-propelled land vehicle in 1769. A heavy front-mounted steam boiler powered two pistons that pushed notched discs attached to the front wheels. The size, placement, and weight of the boiler, however, obscured visibility and made steering difficult and dangerous. Not surprisingly, Cugnot's "car" became the first vehicle involved in a motoring accident; his project was mothballed in 1771.

NELL RICHARDSON   MRS. ALICE BURKE   3806-8

NEW YORK

emperor of China, but it was basically a toy and had no room for a driver. A century later, however, Nicolas-Joseph Cugnot, a French military engineer, designed and built the world's first true automobile—a gigantic, steam-powered tricycle—capable of human transport. Unfortunately, a few years later, Cugnot drove one of his contraptions into a stone wall and became the first person ever injured in an automobile accident. In 1803, Richard Trevithick, who built the world's first steam-engined railway locomotive, drove a vehicle he called the London Steam Carriage from Holborn to Paddington and back, a round trip of about 8 miles. However, the vehicle proved uncomfortable and expensive to operate. In 1808, François Isaac de Rivaz, an inventor and politician, built a vehicle with a primitive hydrogen-fueled engine—often described as the world's first internal combustion powered automobile—but it was never successful. The simple truth was that for comfort,

NELL RICHARDSON AND ALICE BURKE
Sponsored by the National Woman Suffrage Association, Alice Snitzer Burke and Nell Richardson set out on April 6, 1916, on a 10,000-mile trek in support of women's right to vote. Driving their donated Saxon roadster, they gave speeches and interviews, occasionally pulling over for roadside debates with skeptics. Their luggage included a typewriter and a sewing machine. "If any anti-suffragist down in Texas makes remarks about suffrage destroying women's feminine talents," they told a reporter, "it will be Miss Richardson's cue to get out the sewing machine and run off an apron … If, on the other hand, he says women have no brains, she will pull out the typewriter and write him a poem."

economy, and speed, nothing could match a carriage powered by a horse.

The late-nineteenth-century emergence of gasoline-powered automobiles would follow the development of a series of related components, many of them associated with the work of Karl Benz, as he experimented with internal combustion engines. Chief among these were various designs of carburetors to mix petrol and air, a system that would remain in place until the 1980s, when emissions controls and catalytic converters required the greater precision of fuel injection.

Cars didn't merely change the world of travel; they uprooted society, liberating men from their plows and women from their kitchens and washtubs. When, on April 6, 1916, Nell Richardson and Alice Burke departed New York to cross the United States in a donated Saxon roadster, they weren't embarking on a pleasure drive. Armed with a fireless cooker, a hand-operated sewing machine, and a typewriter, they would put some 10,000 miles on their "Golden Flyer" in support of women's suffrage. Along the way, if anti-suffragists complained they were destroying femininity, the pair told a local reporter that Miss Richardson would "get out the sewing machine and run off an apron while the crowd waits."

Thus, the automobile drove social change, playing perhaps history's most significant role in extending and expanding human connectivity. Before 1900, most people still lived on farms in rural communities centered around small towns. Afterward, in a process that continues to this day, paved arteries spread like tentacles across nations to facilitate motorized travel. In turn, these organs of mobility spurred the growth of suburbs, cemented ever-closer connections to and between cities, and, for the first time, enabled truly national systems of commerce. As automotive historian Beverly Rae Kimes has observed, "No other industry, no other entity, combines the sparkling cast of unforgettable

PACKARD
This proud 1934 ragtop exemplifies the thriving Packard Motor Car Company of the 1930s. Offering straight 8 and V-12 cylinder engines, Packard's upscale cars delivered beauty, reliability, and elegance. Though today it might seem politically incorrect, the automaker's signature advertising slogan proclaimed its pride: "Ask the man who owns one."

RUXTON GRIFFIN HOOD ORNAMENT
With improved automotive cooling systems, hood-mounted radiator temperature gauges had all but disappeared by the late 1920s. Especially in prestige vehicles, many so-called "motometers" were replaced by ornaments such as Ruxton's Griffin, which wore the body of a lion and the wings of an eagle, effectively combining the "King of Beasts" with the "King of the Air."

characters, the drama, the comedy, the tragedy, the whole spectrum of life, like the saga of how the world was put on wheels."

At the outset, American manufacturers like Henry Ford and General Motors' William Durant aimed their efforts at the masses. By the 1930s, however, in Europe and the United States,

automakers were bringing luxury, flair, and flamboyance to their creations. America had its coachbuilt Packards, Cadillacs, Duesenbergs, and Pierce-Arrows; England its proud Rolls-Royces and Bentleys; Italy, Germany, and France, swooping and swift Alfa Romeos, Porsches, Bugattis, and Hispano-Suizas. Viewed by the public in magazine advertisements and, later, at car shows around the globe, automotive styling democratized beauty. "It gave us art for the people," said Ken Yohn, a history professor at Kansas's McPherson College, whose curriculum specializes in the restoration of classic vehicles.

In truth, there was nothing new in the celebration of beauteous transport. Shows featuring elegant horse-drawn carriages had begun in France as early as the 1600s. Sundays

1938 H6 HISPANO SUIZA XENIA DUBONNET COUPE
The thirties were a time of experimentation in automotive design and engineering. Nowhere are those trends more evident than in this advanced car by Hispano Suiza, an important aircraft maker in World War I. Actually built to show off its independent front-suspension system (created by race car driver Andre Dubonnet), the Xenia coupe was bodied in the shop of Paris coachbuilder Jacques Saoutchik. Aircraft-like instruments populated its dashboard and the car featured sliding doors, Plexiglass side windows, and a wraparound windshield unseen again until 1950s American automobiles. Power was supplied by an alloy inline six cylinder engine. In 2000, the Xenia coupe won the "Most Elegant Closed Car" award at the Pebble Beach Concours d'Elegance.

became a day for the Parisian elite to parade their wealth and opulence on wheels. "Carriages were gilded, trimmed, and ornamented to an extent never before seen," writes author Abatto. Owners wore the latest fashions and their servants matching livery; "carriages became more sophisticated, coachbuilders introduced open designs, closed designs, and everything in between. These gatherings were, in essence, concours d'elegance, with the general public, who gathered on the sides of roads and on the edges of pathways, serving as spectators."

Similar appreciation would grow as the automobile evolved from a simple box on wheels to an object of desire sculpted in hand-pounded metal. Illustrator and architect Joseph Urban studied at the Academy of Fine Arts in Vienna and was known as an originator of the Art Deco movement. In his own time, however, more

ALFA ROMEO "BAT" CARS

Arguably among history's most flamboyant automotive designs, B.A.T. (Berlina Aerodinamica Technica) cars 5, 7, and 9 were produced by coach builder Bertone in 1953, 1954, and 1955, respectively. Designed by Franco Scaglione, whose work included Alfa's notable gull-wing Stradale 33, Scaglione's daughter Giovanna said her father's cars reflected his dream of "an automobile that, like a falling drop of rainwater… could glide along with only the slightest turbulence and the least friction possible." Auctioned in late 2020 at RM Sotheby's, the cars took less than 10 minutes to achieve a hammer price of more than $14 million.

Americans probably knew him as the designer of the multicolored horizontal bands that embellished the side panels of Ruxton sedans, introduced in 1929. A perfect complement to the car's low-slung silhouette and deco-ish cat's eye headlamps, the flashy accents helped set the

HISPANO SUIZA 'FLYING STORK' HOOD ORNAMENT
For centuries, the white storks of Alsace had been symbols of happiness, fertility, and good luck. When the Germans occupied the region during World War I, French pilots chose the birds as a logo to emblazon the sides of their planes. Hispano-Suiza adopted the bird as a hood ornament both to honor France's flying aces and to mark the firm's own success in building wartime aircraft engines. The ornament is considered one of the most beautiful of its type ever created.

pioneering front-wheel-drive cars apart, though not enough to save them from the ravages of the Great Depression.

Despite such economic difficulties, the years between World Wars I and II saw an explosion of creative styling, what many still regard as a golden age of automotive design. Artisans such as French coachbuilders Giuseppe Figoni and Ovidio Falaschi were deeply influenced by the shapes of airplanes and the impact of the wind (though, unlike modern-day designers, they lacked access to wind tunnels or computers). The pontoon fenders on Figoni and Falaschi cars such as the 1936 Delahaye 135 and the 1938 Talbot-Lago T 150 coupe reflected their mutual fascination with teardrop shapes. The 1938 Hispano Suiza Dubbonet Xenia scaled a similar interwar peak. The brainchild of World War I flying ace and inventor André Dubbonet, the Xenia was actually built to demonstrate a new suspension system. Like other coachbuilt cars of its time, however, the coupe's lines flowed like droplets driven by the wind.

Indeed, some twenty years later, Italian designer Franco Scaglione revealed the extent of such influences in his famous B.A.T. cars for Alfa Romeo. "Pencil in his left hand," he "drew the shapes his mind visualized," according to interviews with the designer's daughter, Giovanna. "His dream was of an automobile that, like a falling drop of rainwater in the air, could glide along with only the slightest turbulence and with the least friction possible, a car that could travel quickly without disturbing the outside air." Though distinctly futuristic in their sweeping fins that curl like ocean waves and Xenia-reminiscent triangular rear windows, Scaglione's B.A.T. cars echoed the seminal automotive shapes of the 1930s. Hints of such elements can also be seen in cars such as 1963's Corvette Sting Ray split-window coupe.

As did the car itself, the activities surrounding the automobile had a democratizing effect. At its formation on June 20, 1904, the Federation Internationale de l'Automobile pledged to "represent the interests of motoring organizations and motor car users." The excitement generated by events like the London to Brighton run, the Paris to Bordeaux race, and, beginning in 1929, Italy's Concorso d'Eleganza Villa d'Este soon spread. The handbuilt craftmanship of earlier cars as well as the skill involved in keeping them running became widely celebrated. American men in the 1920 and '30s began disappearing from dinner tables to tinker in their garages. In 1935, the Antique Automobile Club of America was formed; the postwar era saw the birth of the Classic Car Club of America in 1952 and in Europe and America, marque clubs sprang up

MAGAZINE SPREAD
Specialty auto-enthusiast magazines became popular following World War II, at least partly inspired by the fondness of America's returning servicemen for British sports cars. *Road & Track*, for example, was founded in June 1947, and later sold to CBS Publications in 1972. In 2019, the magazine moved to New York where, along with its sister, *Car and Driver*, it is still published by Hearst Corporation.

where owners with similar interests could share knowledge and socialize. It was a time of square-dancing, fox-tail stoles, Crosley radios, and specialty car magazines.

As appreciation for automotive beauty spread, so too did the custom of formal car shows. While the world's first car show had occurred in Paris in 1894, and America's initial display of new automobiles came at New York's Madison Square Garden on November 3, 1900, the first showing of vintage automobiles was at the Concorso d'Eleganza Villa d'Este, which debuted at Lake Como, Italy, in September 1929. It would be twenty years before the first North American concours d'elegance was held at Pebble Beach, California, in 1950.

That show came as a last-minute adjunct to the Pebble Beach Road Race—the first race sponsored by the new Sports Car Club of America. The twisty course down the Monterey Peninsula's 17-Mile Drive challenged drivers to pilot some of the world's fastest sports cars through high-speed turns, often while coping with near-nonexistent visibility. Either the road was shrouded by fog, slickened by rain, or, as remembered by Pebblebeach.com in 2019, blinded by brilliant sunshine that spiked between the trees like flashing strobes of light. "Modest stacks of hay bales buffeted the course," the website went on, "serving as a last line of defense—both for the fans packed ten rows deep, sometimes just 10 yards off the course,

PEBBLE BEACH TOUR D' ELEGANCE
As a prelude to Sunday's world-famous show, on Thursday 100 or more entrants prove their roadworthiness by tracing a route along and around California's scenic Highway One. Many of the cars return to park along Carmel's Ocean Avenue where they are mobbed by onlookers—no touching, please!—free of charge. A car that successfully completes the tour gets the nod if it later ties in class competition at the Concours.

and for the daring drivers spinning out of control toward a forest of tree trunks."

Phil Hill, who would later become the only American-born driver to capture the Formula One World Driver's championship, won the initial race. Six years later, Carroll Shelby won the final Pebble Beach Road Race, which was permanently canceled after a fatal crash. In 1957, the race moved to purpose-built track at nearby Laguna Seca. Meanwhile, the Pebble Beach Concours d'Elegance has continued, with the exception of cancellations in 1960 due to scheduling conflicts and the impact of the 2020 pandemic.

Today, Pebble Beach remains arguably the world's premier showplace for the display and celebration of vintage automobiles. Up to 20,000 spectators pay from $400 to $3,500 to attend the single-day event, itself the culmination of what has become a ten-day "Car Week" that includes a half dozen major auctions, as well as

PEBBLE BEACH RUSSO AND STEELE AUCTION
A major feature of Monterey County, California's annual Car Week are its many car auctions. Indeed, according to the *New York Times*, between 2010 and the onset of 2020's pandemic, the area's auctions generated more than $3 billion in sales—the most of any live car auctions in America.

TOP COLLECTOR CAR SHOWS: A SAMPLING

MARCH	Amelia Island Concours d'Elegance, Amelia Island, Florida
MAY	Concorso d'Eleganza, Villa d'Este, Lake Como, Italy
JUNE	Greenwich Concours d'Elegance, Greenwich, Connecticut
JULY	Hillsborough Concours d'Elegance, Hillsborough, California
	Chantilly Arts & Elegance Concours, Chateau de Chantilly, France (biennial)
AUGUST	Pebble Beach Concours d'Elegance, Pebble Beach, California
SEPTEMBER	Concours of Elegance, Hampton Court Palace, England
	Salon Privé Concours d'Elegance, Oxfordshire, England
	Goodwood Revival, Chichester, England
OCTOBER	AACA Eastern Fall Meet, Hershey, Pennsylvania
	Audrain's Newport Concours & Motor Week, Newport, Rhode Island
NOVEMBER	Hilton Head Island Concours, Hilton Head Island, South Carolina

TOP CAR MUSEUMS: A SAMPLING

UNITED STATES

America's Car Museum, Tacoma, Washington

Blackhawk Museum, Danville, California

The Henry Ford Museum, Dearborn, Michigan

Indianapolis Motor Speedway Hall of Fame Museum, Speedway, Indiana

Petersen Automotive Museum, Los Angeles, California

Audrain Museum, Newport, Rhode Island

Simeone Foundation Automotive Museum, Philadelphia, Pennsylvania

The Revs Institute (Collier Collection), Naples, Florida

Antique Automobile Club of America Museum, Hershey, Pennsylvania

Larz Anderson Auto Museum, Brookline, Massachusetts

The Nethercutt Collection, Sylmar, California

EUROPE

Cité de l'Automobile, Mulhouse, France

Mercedes-Benz Museum, Stuttgart, Germany

The Porsche Museum, Stuttgart, Germany

Alfa Romeo Museum, Milan, Italy

British Motor Museum, Gaydon, Warwickshire, England

Haynes Motor Museum, Somerset, England

separate shows for German and Italian vehicles, small cars, and automotive oddities and misfits. The week's auctions routinely generate hundreds of millions in collectible car sales; the Pebble Beach show alone contributes some $2 million a year to charity.

Younger collectors, meanwhile, are fostering new, more inclusive, and less conventional venues for displaying their vehicles. "RADwood" events, for example, are self-described celebrations of 1980s and 1990s "automotive lifestyles." Open to cars, trucks, and motorcycles from those decades, they feature music from the era and owner-participants wearing period-correct attire. (Think *Miami Vice*, mullets, or perhaps an 8-ball jacket.) RADwood shows have been staged throughout the country, including during

LUFTGEKÜHLT
Increasingly popular "happenings" for younger owners of air-cooled Porsches, these events have been called "The hottest ticket in auto enthusiasm," by *Autoweek*. Thousands of Stuttgart air-breathers—in conditions ranging from pristine to putrid—descended upon a recent Luftgekühlt event in Hollywood, zipping around tinsel town and visiting studios. The above gathering happened in 2019 in San Pedro, California.

Carmel's Car Week. Not to be outdone, Porsche owners congregate by the hundreds for semi spontaneous Luftgekühlt ("air-cooled") events—called "the hottest ticket in auto enthusiasm" by *Autoweek*—which are open to all models of the make, and in conditions varying from world class to beaters. In many respects, RADwood and Luftgekühlt are as much happenings as car shows.

For seeing rare cars in fully restored condition, it is hard to beat the growing number of specialized museums in the United States and Europe, most of them built by wealthy collectors or automakers in the years since World War II.

Before there were large-scale classic car shows and public auctions—let alone the internet—vintage automobiles were bought and sold by word of mouth or via advertisements printed in club newsletters, local newspapers, and enthusiast publications like *Hemmings Motor News.* Max Hoffman's Park Avenue dealership in New York led the way in bringing European cars to America after World War II. Specialized dealers like Fantasy Junction and Heritage Classics in Emeryville and West Hollywood, California, respectively; Hyman Ltd., in St. Louis, Missouri; and many others followed—offering mostly vintage European sports cars—as early as the 1970s. "Interest in antique automobiling has grown in phenomenal proportion and rapidity in the last ten years," wrote Scott and Margaret Bailey in the 1958 handbook *Buy an Antique Car.* "Cars that today are deemed priceless antiques were, a few years ago, laid to the cutting torch." To today's collector, of course, those late-1950s "priceless" prices seem an unbelievable bargain.

In 1996, however, when the two-year-old cablevision network Speedvision launched taped coverage of the Barrett-Jackson auction in Scottsdale, Arizona, the buying and selling of vintage cars was transformed. "We pulled phenomenal ratings," Craig Jackson later recalled to a television interviewer. "It was groundbreaking, and changed the world of car collecting forever. It brought new blood into the hobby—we put this on television and it just kicked the doors down." In 1997, the Barrett Jackson Speedvision telecast would go live and, within a few years, classic car auctions would routinely be televised, often with phone-in bidders competing from around the globe.

A decade later, the buying and selling of collectible cars would convulse again, and this time the internet would play the starring role. Leading the charge would be Bring-a-Trailer.com, a fast-growing website that, by the dawn of the 2020s, counted two million monthly visitors and 100,000 registered bidders. Known as "BaT" and housed in a former brick warehouse in San Francisco's Potrero Hill District, the site saw its sales jump 41 percent in 2019, to $230 million then just keep climbing. When the coronavirus epidemic swept the planet in 2020, BaT proved its true mettle, with sales topping $400 million, a 60-plus percent leap. "Nobody knew what would happen in March or April," Randy Nonnenberg, the site's cofounder and president told the *New York Times* in November 2021, "but in the past nine months many people tasted and tested what it was like to transact online in a socially restricted environment. They now see this as a useful and effective way to pursue their interests, including collectible cars." As 2022 dawned, the website reported its previous year had nudged $1 billion—$829 million, to be exact.

A passion that began on unpaved roads in the nineteenth century went on to endure global wars, economic downturns, and two pandemics, and it appears robust enough to survive the coming decade and beyond. In the end, car collecting is not about cars but about people. As Spencer Trenery, president of Fantasy Junction, put it, "When COVID came along, so much of life moving forward became unknown. People looking at a car they'd wanted for years asked: 'If not now, when?'" As the world continued on an uncertain path in the 2020s, that question seemed more relevant than ever.

2

CONSOLIDATION AND QUALITY

How car making changed, eventually yielding a new era of precision and reliability.

1895 DURYEA MOTOR WAGON
With a single cylinder, 4 horsepower engine, the Duryea was the first gasoline-powered automobile built and sold in the U.S. Duryeas won America's first road race and the first London to Brighton run, capturing the latter event by more than an hour.

"To rush through the air at the speed of a torpedo-boat destroyer, down a narrow, curving road, enclosed with hedges, and without being able to see what was to the front of us, was a novel and thrilling experience. The slightest error of steering would have landed us into one bank or the other, or plunged us into the midst of cyclists who were waiting at the bottom of the hill to see how we should take this admittedly awkward piece of country. We did it magnificently, without a swerve, and all the while our motor was actively impelling us onward, adding to the velocity which had been already imparted to the vehicle by the momentum. It was a grand sensation, and the danger of the feat was not lessened by a rearing horse attached to a cart which we narrowly shaved at the foot of the hill, and which we had calculated would involve us all in utter wreck and discomfiture."

From a passenger's eyewitness report of the first London to Brighton "Emancipation" Run in 1896.

LOHNER-PORSCHE MIXED HYBRID
Produced from 1900–1905, the Lohner-Porsche "Mixte" was the world's first gasoline-electric hybrid vehicle. Ferdinand Porsche used a petrol-fueled generator to supply electric motors mounted at each wheel hub. Although its weight and short range eventually doomed the first "Mixte," more than a century later Porsche resurrected the concept of shared-fuel electromobility with the Cayenne S Hybrid.

N otably, that first race in far-off England was won by an American-made Duryea Motor Wagon, which beat its closest arrivals to Brighton by more than an hour. Indeed, the year before Duryea had captured its home country's first automobile race—a 52.4-mile event that started and ended in Chicago. By 1896, brothers Frank and Charles Duryea had built thirteen cars at their 47 Taylor Street factory in Springfield, Massachusetts, making their horseless carriage the first commercially produced automobile in the United States.

The Duryea Motor Wagon Company went bankrupt two years later. But by the late nineteenth century, in hundreds of American barns and garages, engines were being invented, manufactured, and installed in formerly horse-powered conveyances. By the first post-1900 years, nearly 2,000 automotive companies had been formed, producing some 3,000 makes. Together, according to the New England Auto Museum, they'd managed to sell some 4,200 new automobiles in the United States.

Gasoline powered fewer than 1,000 of those cars, the Burlington, Connecticut-based museum estimated. In fact, the 160 vehicles

at the nation's first automobile show—held in New York City's Madison Square Garden on November 3, 1900—displayed "an innovative assortment of electric, steam, and 'internal explosion' engines." The low regard in which the latter were held was reflected in scathing descriptors flung by contemporary critics: "Noxious, noisy, unreliable, and elephantine. It vibrates so violently as to loosen one's dentures," said one. The air, complained another, was "ruthlessly spoiled by the large number of petrol engines in use."

In fact, if anything was explosive in those early days, it was innovation itself. In 1901, Ferdinand Porsche, later father of the Volkswagen Beetle, created the first gasoline-electric hybrid vehicle at the Jakob Lohner & Company factory in Vienna. Rather than a massive battery, the "Lohner-Porsche Mixte Hybrid" employed a setup not unlike 2022's Mazda's MX-30 plug-in hybrid in which a gasoline-powered rotary engine serves as a range extender for EV operation. In the century-old German car, an internal combustion engine powered a generator that in turn drove electric motors at the hub of each wheel. Thus, Porsche's "Mixte" became not only the first hybrid, but also the first all-wheel-drive car. It should be noted that electric vehicles possessed a major advantage over gasoline-powered cars of the time, especially among women drivers: electric starters—Henry Ford's wife Clara drove an electric car until 1914. After doing away with the hand crank, gasoline cars powered past electrics for good by the 1920s. Detroit Electric, the last of its breed, ceased operation in 1939.

Early on, steam offered a popular alternative to both electric and gasoline cars. According to *The Complete Encyclopedia of Motorcars* (Ebury Press, 1973), more than half of U.S. new car registrations in 1902 were for steam-powered cars. Steamers were mostly safe, fast, quiet, and reliable. However, buyers soon learned that early steam cars required heavy heating boilers, considerable attention, and frequent stops for water—the latter often necessitating pauses at local horse troughs. Like electric cars, steamers eventually gave way to gasoline; not even automated, quick-firing boilers could save them. By 1920, only three steam carmakers were still in business: Stanley and Conrad lasted until 1924, and Doble closed its doors in 1930 after building only thirty-six cars in the preceding eight years. Though sporadic attempts would be made to revive steam-powered cars in coming decades—including by aviation pioneer William Lear in 1973—none would survive beyond the testing stage.

CITA NO. 25
On April 25, 1899, outside Paris, the alloy-bodied CITA No. 25, driven by Belgian race car driver Camille Jenatzy, became the first vehicle to exceed 100 kilometers (62 miles) per hour. The torpedo-shaped vehicle was powered by two 25 kilowatt electric motors.

The first sports cars debuted during the early "brass" era, with England's first Morgan three-wheel cyclecar in 1909, America's Mercer Raceabout in 1910, and France's Bugatti Type 13 in 1910.

Technological advances came rapidly after 1920. Engines expanded to V-8, V-12, and V-16 configurations, with some boasting multivalve and overhead camshaft designs. Duesenberg unveiled four-wheel hydraulic brakes in 1921, and front-wheel drive was pioneered by Ruxton and Cord passenger cars at the dawn of the 1930s.

At the same time, however, economies of scale and mass production chipped away at the number of automakers. In the three years between 1922 and 1925, for example, ninety-five American carmakers disappeared, leaving only seventy in operation. The 1930s saw impressive strides in design—fully enclosed bodies with integrated fenders and enclosed storage trunks big enough for a spare tire, for example—but the Great Depression further winnowed the number of automakers. Duesenberg, Pierce Arrow, Cord, Auburn, Stutz, Marmon, Cunningham, and Peerless—and the independent coachbuilders who'd supplied bespoke bodies for their chassis—were among the casualties. Independents like Packard, Hudson, Crosley, and Nash survived the war, but only until the 1950s. Meanwhile, the Big Three thrived. Ford, which had purchased Lincoln

HUDSON HORNET
The Hudson Motor Car Company's slick cornering "step-down" design and its big six-cylinder engine helped the Hornet dominate early 1950s NASCAR racing. Indeed, Hudson Hornets won 108 races between 1951 and 1953. Special exterior badging (shown below) distinguished the speedy models but—like most postwar independent automakers—Hudson couldn't stave off consolidation with Nash a few years later.

in 1922, launched the mid-price Mercury in 1939. General Motors, formed in 1908 through the acquisition of Buick, Oldsmobile, and what became Pontiac, bought Cadillac a year later. In 1918, GM bought Chevrolet—cofounded by William Durant and Swiss race car driver Louis Chevrolet five years earlier. Last but by no means least, in 1925, Walter Chrysler reorganized and renamed the Maxwell Motor Company as Chrysler Corporation. He acquired Dodge in 1927 and introduced the Plymouth and DeSoto brands a year later.

After World War II, the remaining independents were forced to combine or fold. Despite still outselling Cadillac and having built a long-standing reputation for quality and reliability, Packard steadily lost ground as the 1950s unfolded. Its newly developed Ultramatic transmission couldn't match the

STUDEBAKER AVANTI
Studebaker and Packard merged in hopes of surviving the 1950s but the venerable Packard name died in 1958. Four years later, Studebaker pinned its last hopes on the stylish, Raymond Loewy–designed Avanti, among the world's fastest production cars at the time. Although Studebaker folded in 1966 after 114 years in business, Avantis continued to be built by small, independent automakers until 2006.

smoothness of GM's Hydramatic, and its venerable straight-eight was perceived as dated compared to its rival's overhead valve V-8's. Even so, the venerable "ask the man who drives one" company responded with a competitive V-8 and was still financially viable when it acquired Studebaker Corporation in 1954. Unfortunately, despite its flashy line of two-door Hawk sports cars, the South Bend, Indiana, automaker was a financial basket case. By

1949 DELAHAYE 175 S ROADSTER BY SAOUTCHIK
An elaboration of the Figoni and Falaschi designed "narwhal" Delahayes, the 175 S by Ukrainian-born Jacques Saoutchik featured bold masses of chrome and fully skirted wheel openings that imparted a dazzling sense of length, grace, and speed. The S featured triple Solex carburetors, fully independent suspension, and a newly designed 4.5-liter, six-cylinder engine with seven main bearings. Along with Talbot Lago, the 175 was among the last of the great postwar French luxury cars.

1957, the flailing victim had sucked the life out of its intended rescuer-host. Not even Packard's industry-leading Torsion-Level suspension system could save the doughty marque.

At the same time, American Motors' hopes of bringing Studebaker Packard Co. into its fold—and thereby enlarging the industry Big Three to a Big Four—stalled out after AMC merged Nash, Hudson, and later acquired Jeep from Kaiser Willys. Studebaker enjoyed a last gasp with its stunning, Raymond Loewy–designed Avanti, the world's fastest production car when it was introduced in 1963. But the final Studebaker-built Avantis only lasted through the following year; the company itself died in Canada in 1966.

After shedding its struggling performers, America's postwar automotive industry mushroomed into a colossus, selling nearly 60 million cars between 1950 and 1960. And with each year's introduction of new models, the vehicles it produced grew flashier and longer. Every fall, the race quickened for more horsepower and chrome, fancier interiors, and more amenities like FM radios and air-conditioning. The problem: quality and reliability suffered, at least partly by design. The process became known as "planned obsolescence," and its champion was Alfred P. Sloan Jr., General Motors' CEO from 1923 until 1956. As Sloan explained in his 1963 autobiography, *My Years with General Motors*, "The [annual] changes in the new model should be so novel and attractive as to create demand . . . and a certain amount of dissatisfaction with past models as compared with the new one." Industry maverick John DeLorean, father of GM's Ferrari-memorializing Pontiac GTO and later his own gull-wing DeLorean, had a different view: "Here I was spending my life bending the fenders a little differently to try to convince the public they were getting a new and

engineered. In the mid-1950s, for example, Alfa Romeo launched a revolutionary new series of four-cylinder, all-aluminum, overhead cam engines that offered surprising quickness and reliability. Porsche's durable flat-four, air-cooled engine provided similar performance. Mercedes debuted fuel injection in the 1950s in its top-tier 300 SL sports cars; in England, Jaguar was winning Le Mans races while Morris Garage and its ubiquitous TC, TD, and TF sports cars invaded American college campuses, brought home by returning GIs who'd fallen in love with the fun little roadsters from England.

TALBOT LAGO T150 TEARDROP COUPE
Here shown at the Pebble Beach Concours d'Elegance, Figoni & Falaschi's Teardrop Coupes were considered among the finest expressions of 1930s French streamlined design. Only sixteen of the teardrops were ultimately built. In 2022 at Amelia Island, Florida, Gooding & Co. auctioned a 1937 T150 for $13.4 million, making it the most expensive French car ever publicly sold and setting a world record for the marque.

dramatically different product," he complained. "What gross excesses! Engineering had become a wing of marketing. It was ridiculous."

At the same time, postwar European cars had become faster, cheaper to drive, and, many enthusiasts argued, better made and

For the most part, European cars were built differently. Since the 1920s, construction of American autos had followed the body-on-frame approach used in making horseless carriages; the vehicle's body sat on a ladder-like frame. Though initially the frames were made of ash, manufacturers soon switched to steel. The system had advantages—the metal frame resisted twisting, bending, and breaking, was therefore damage-resistant in accidents or rough terrain, and was well-suited for truck applications where heavy load–carrying capability was a key requirement. The design also aided automakers in making annual body style changes, including modifications to provide a softer ride, by allowing greater wheel travel and larger tires, for example. Ford's venerable Crown Victoria and Lincoln Town Cars rode on body-on-frame platforms until the early 2000s. Today, many SUV and pickup models, including those offered by Toyota, Lexus, etc., still utilize body-on-frame designs.

By contrast, many European automakers adopted unibody or monocoque construction. Although some credit the 1930s Chrysler Airstream with this achievement, historians believe the technique was introduced by Lancia more than a decade earlier. In any event, the new design did away with heavy steel rails in favor of integrating the car's frame and body in a single piece. The approach sharply reduced vehicle weight, ensuring better fuel economy, and made it possible to shape the car closer to its key components, making it smaller and more aerodynamic and imparting improved road handling. Many European cars also featured rack-and-pinion steering, which greatly increased the sense of tightness and accuracy in steering. Finally, monocoque construction made easier the inclusion of "crumple zones" that—while not preventing damage—could better absorb the force of a crash and thus provide greater occupant safety.

As the 1960s dawned—and well into the 1970s—European cars often simply felt better made. Gaps around doors, trunks, and engine bonnets were typically tighter than in American automobiles. Proud new Ferrari or Mercedes owners might tell an envious friend to listen for the solid, vault-like click when they opened and closed the vehicle's doors. Or point to the burnished wood surrounding the car's purposeful instrument panel, which typically included a tachometer and oil pressure gauge, devices usually absent from Detroit vehicles. Or show off the interior's supple and carefully sewn Connolly leather. In Mercedes's case, even the MB-Tex vinyl upholstery used in the firm's sports cars always seemed to look new and last longer than typical U.S.-sourced material.

Part of the reason for the perceived differences in quality may have been the continued presence in Europe of *carrozzeria* (or coachbuilding). There, even at the twentieth century's halfway point, coachbuilding—that is, the fashioning and assembly of car bodies by hand—was still practiced and revered. In comparison, by the end of the 1930s, American coachbuilders like Dietrich Inc. (Packard), LeBaron (Chrysler), Murphy (Buick), and Rollston (Duesenberg) had mostly disappeared or been absorbed by corporate automakers. Not so in England (Park Ward), France (Henri Chapron, Figoni et Falaschi), Germany (Karmann), and especially Italy. Founded in 1919, for example, Zagato bodied cars for Alfa Romeo, Ferrari, Lancia, Lamborghini, Maserati, Porsche, and Aston Martin, and is still operated by the same family today. However, by 1970 even most European coachbuilders—firms like Vignale, Ghia, and Touring (famous for its lightweight Superleggera designs)—had gone out of business.

It would take a newcomer to the international automotive scene, and the theories of a then-obscure American, to reinstill a devotion to quality in automaking. The newcomer was postwar Japan Inc., and the American was a Yale-trained engineer named W. Edwards Deming. Together, they would fundamentally change how cars were manufactured. And today, what they accomplished presents a rare opportunity for NextGen collectors (more about that later).

For Japanese automakers, the climb to respectability had been agonizingly slow. "For a long time after World War II, Japanese cars borrowed engine designs and styling cues from American firms like Ford and General Motors," Ed Loh, editor in chief of *MotorTrend*, told the *New York Times* in October 2019. Unlike European automakers, which quickly reestablished their prewar reputations for craftsmanship, "Made in Japan" largely existed as a pejorative, synonymous with cheap manufacturing methods and flimsy construction. Indeed, some companies deliberately located factories in the Japanese city of Usa, so their products could be stamped "Made in USA."

Mr. Loh and others believe a major factor in turning that image around—and a key underlying element in the current surge in Japanese cars' collectability—were the theories of a man who'd been largely ignored in his own country.

Armed with a Ph.D. in mathematical physics, Dr. Deming advocated the use of statistical analysis to improve manufacturing quality and efficiency. Rather than inspect products for defects after they were made, he urged a continual approach that involved every worker from the beginning. Dr. Deming called for scrutinizing each step of production with the goal of achieving *kaizen*, a Japanese word that refers to the improvement of all processes by involving every employee, from a company's top ranks to its assembly-line workers.

W. EDWARDS DEMING
Armed with a Yale Ph.D. in mathematical physics, Deming advocated the use of statistical analysis to improve manufacturing quality and efficiency. He urged scrutinizing each step of production to achieve *kaizen*, a Japanese word meaning the improvement of all processes by involving every employee. Dr. Deming was awarded the Second Order Medal of the Sacred Treasure by Japanese Emperor Hirohito in 1960. Below, he is seen at a Toyota facility in November, 1970.

Datsun built the 240-Z for connoisseur drivers who appreciate a luxuriously appointed high performance sports car.

A car that fulfils your most exacting desire for excellence. A true Gran Turismo. Superb styling. Thrilling performance. (SS ¼ mile in 16.5 secs. and top speed of 125 m.p.h.) Advanced safety engineering. Outstanding handling.

2400 cc. 150 h.p. 6-cylinder overhead cam mill; twin SU-type carbs; aircraft-style cockpit and instrument panel; road hugging all-independent suspension; radial tyres; all synchro 5-speed stick shift; power assisted brakes, disc-front, drum-rear. face-level flow-through ventilation; auto-tune radio with power antenna.

Every extra at no extra cost . . . that's the nice part!

Datsun 240-Z at your Datsun Dealer.

Nissan Motor Co. Ltd.

For those who know and love a fine-tuned thoroughbred

Introducing Datsun 240 Z

DATSUN 240Z

Introduced in the U.S. in 1970, the 240 Z became Japan's first high-volume sports car. The Z car had it all, said *MotorTrend*: performance, reliability, and an affordable price tag. Echoing Jaguar's more costly E-type, the Japanese car offered a long hood, an overhead-cam six, a four-speed transmission, and a full set of gauges—in other words, real sports car credentials.

Starting in 1950, Dr. Deming urged Japanese companies to adopt this philosophy, which he called "continual improvement." Using statistical tools, he said, workers should monitor each step in the assembly process with the goal of meeting a series of quality standards. However, he also strongly advocated eliminating quotas and sloganeering and urged an inclusive approach to employees, one in which rewards for success were shared by teams, not individuals. Dr. Deming fervently believed that every worker had nearly unlimited potential when placed in an environment that "adequately supports, educates, and nurtures [his or her] senses of pride and responsibility."

"In the United States, Deming initially was viewed as an oddball mathematician," said Jack Keebler, a Detroit-based automotive journalist and former quality-review team leader for General Motors. "American car companies in the 1950s and '60s had little competition and Japan was regarded as a place where they made funny little cars that looked like toys. But the Japanese companies, especially Toyota, were taking the Deming strictures to heart."

Then, as Mr. Keebler put it, "the switch got flipped." Americans started to realize that weird little cars like the Datsun F10 were going 70,000 miles without needing a brake job or their valves reground. "The plastics might die early," Mr. Keebler noted, "but the engine blocks and cylinder heads were of very good integrity. A Japanese car wouldn't leave you stranded beside the road." By comparison, an American car with 100,000 miles was considered to have reached a milestone. "And by then it might have had a transmission overhaul and its brakes and a cylinder head replaced."

In 1970, Nissan introduced the 240Z and took the car world for a spin. "The difference between the Datsun 240Z and your everyday three-and-a-half-thousand dollar sports car is that about twice as much thinking went into the Datsun," enthused *Car and Driver* at the time.

"It shows. Datsun didn't invent the overhead cam engine, or disc brakes, or independent suspension, but it has a habit of incorporating these sophisticated systems into brilliantly conceived and easily affordable cars."

The article went on to rate the "Z-car" as "several" miles per hour faster than a 2-liter Porsche 911T; quicker in a quarter mile than a Triumph TR6; superior to "whimsical, superficial cars like the Opel GT"; and able to "keep right up with your neighbor's Bonneville." At least as important, the Datsun was "kind" to its driver. "The steering effort is moderate; the shifting motions are light and acceptably precise; and the driving position is excellent," declared the reviewer.

On June 24, 1980, NBC televised a documentary titled "If Japan Can . . . Why Can't We?" about the leaps being made by Nippon's automakers. For the first time, millions of viewers were introduced to Dr. Deming as the American widely credited with the Japanese automotive resurgence. He was persona obscura no more. Already honored by the emperor of Japan, W. Edwards Deming, who died in 1993, would go on to receive the National Medal of Technology from President Reagan in 1987 and the National Academy of Sciences Distinguished Career in Science award in 1988. He was inducted into the Automotive Hall of Fame in 1991.

"After the NBC show, he was in constant demand," recalled Bill Scherkenbach, a New York University graduate business student when he first met Dr. Deming in 1972. The older man was a visiting lecturer teaching statistical analysis and sampling. The two hit it off and Mr. Scherkenbach soon joined his former professor on consulting trips around the globe. When Ford Motor Company came calling for full-time help, Dr. Deming recommended his former student, who was appointed director of statistical methods under COO (and subsequent CEO) Don Petersen.

"Quality is made at the top," said Mr. Scherkenbach in an interview. "As Dr. Deming would say, 'Management is prediction.' He did not suffer fools, especially CEOs who thought they knew everything. But he could also be endlessly patient and compassionate with those who wanted to learn. . . . If there's fear in an organization, you can't trust the data. You must understand the power of intrinsic motivation and how to help people take joy in their work."

When Mr. Scherkenbach arrived at Ford, the company had separate engine and transmission divisions whose managers were evaluated—and rewarded—based on the performance of their individual groups. Thus, because relatively inexpensive quality improvements could raise a unit's costs and thereby negatively impact a performance evaluation, managers all too often decided against changes that may have reduced or avoided far higher costs for the company as a whole. The issue was eventually resolved by unifying the groups in a combined power train division. In addition, personnel evaluation was given a broader, longer-term focus; for example, come managers' retirement compensations were partly based on how their group performed *after* they'd left their jobs.

By the 1990s, Japan's automakers had fully mastered the art and science of unibody construction. With serial luxury car introductions by Honda's Acura, Nissan's Infiniti, and Toyota's Lexus divisions, Japanese vehicles had put the world on notice. "I remember test-driving those early Lexus sedans and coupes for the first time," recalled Mr. Keebler. "Even compared to premium German cars, they were dazzlingly smooth-riding and silent-running. I knew instantly that something seismic had happened in the automotive universe."

Welding techniques and adhesives had received step-by-step Deming-driven improvements. Shut lines of doors, trunk lids, and hoods were tighter. Window glass was thicker and body paint shinier. Engines and drivetrains had achieved new levels of precision. Japan, and especially Toyota, took Deming's ideas about continual improvement seriously and implemented them. With their extra strong bodies and mechanical refinements, the cars rode smoother and quieter, handled better, and were more reliable. "Detroit had to work very hard to catch up," said Mr. Keebler.

The payoff for today's enthusiasts and collectors is that even high-mileage, decades-old Japanese cars offer dependable fun. Recent online ads for thirty-year-old Nissan 300 ZX sports cars are a good example. One well-kept 1992 model with 99,000 miles had an asking price of $35,000; a 1991 turbo-equipped ZX sought $23,000 despite showing 187,000 miles.

Many collectible high-mileage Japanese cars remain available at attractive prices. In 2021, Bring-a-Trailer.com recorded Acura NSX sales ranging from $159,000 for a 1993 model with a mere 3,500 miles to $43,000 for an ultra clean, all-records '91 showing 159,000 miles. "If the car's current mileage is causing anyone to hesitate placing a bid, don't let it," urged an NSX-owning BaT commenter during bidding. "Honda doesn't consider an NSX engine broken in until it has reached the 70,000-mile mark. These cars are so special they defy description. They were meant to be driven."

Among the biggest bangs for an enthusiast's affordable buck are Mazda Miatas—the world's most mass-produced sports cars—though current prices, especially for mint first-generation cars, appear to be climbing.

"We never thought we were building a collectible car," said Tom Matano, executive director of the School of Industrial Design at San Francisco's Academy of Art University. Leader of Miata's original design team, Mr. Matano recalled being inspired by small English roadsters such as MGs, Triumphs, and Austin-Healeys.

1996 LEXUS SC 300
"When we applied the Deming methods to our system, they created a truly transformative virtuous circle," Paul Williamsen, strategic communication manager for Lexus International, recalled in the *New York Times*. Introduced at the beginning of the 1990s, the Lexus SC coupes exhibited a host of Deming-driven improvements. Shut lines of doors, trunk lids, and hoods were tighter. Window glass was thicker and body paint shinier. Engines and drivetrains had achieved new levels of internal precision. As a result, even high-mileage, decades-old Japanese cars can supply today's enthusiast with dependable fun. The SC 300 shown has 250,000 miles and still wears its original paint and interior leather.

Early Miatas are included in what Hagerty defines as "up-and-coming" collectibles, based on final sales and sell-through rates at live (as opposed to online) auctions. Other models, mostly from the 1990s, on the list: Mazda RX-7; Accura Integra Type R; Toyota Supra and MR2; Nissan 300ZX; and Honda S2000.

As a group, the up-and-comers' final auction prices and sell-through rates averaged $31,173 and 62 percent, respectively, in 2018. A year later, those figures had jumped to $43,403 and 74 percent, Brian Rabold, then editor of Hagerty's price guide, told the *New York Times* in November 2019. "The new collectible market is being driven by millennials," he said. "If a young person is only going to have one fun car, these Japanese models are familiar, usable, and affordable. They check all the boxes."

Millennials also dominate the lesser-known "JDM" collector cars, Mr. Rabold added. These are right-hand-drive vehicles that were built for the Japanese domestic market. Because of a U.S. law that bans their import for twenty-five years—except for "show and display"—JDM models such as the Nissan Skyline, Mitsubishi Pajero, and Honda City Turbo are only now becoming available Stateside.

As the reader may have gathered, 1990s Japanese cars represent a market sweet spot for thrifty NextGen buyers. As Mr. Keebler said, "There's still a window to get in at reasonable prices, but the cat is coming out of the bag with Japanese cars. Their quality is going to validate their collectability."

The good news is that European and American cars got better too in the post-Deming period; we'll highlight some especially attractive NextGen candidates in coming chapters. After all, doesn't it say something that quality champion Mr. Scherkenbach, Dr. Deming's erstwhile disciple, advocate, and global consulting companion, drives the most popular vehicle of all time, a Ford F-150?

Below:
FERRARI 250 GTO
Dubbed the "world's most important, desirable and legendary automobile," by RM Sotheby's, the 250 GTO has the distinction of being one of the most expensive cars ever sold, either privately or publicly. WeatherTech founder David MacNeil paid $70 million in a private treaty transaction and another 250 crossed the block for $48.4 million at Sotheby's Monterey, Calif auction, both in 2018. Here, a GTO competes at the Louis Vuitton Classic.

3

INVESTING

MOST EXPENSIVE CAR EVER
The ultra-rare 1955 Mercedes-Benz 300 SLR Uhlenhaut Coupe was purchased for $142.9 million by an anonymous bidder at an invitation-only factory auction managed by RM Sotheby's. The racer also ranked among the 10 most expensive items of any kind sold at auction, RM Sotheby's said.

"I was dubious that old Ferraris would ever be a good investment and passed up five 250 GTOs going for around $5,000 to $9,000."

Dick Merritt, former editor of *The Prancing Horse*, Ferrari Club of America magazine, recalling regrettable late-1960s decisions.

ORIGINAL FERRARI LIST PRICES:

1959 Type 250 Testa Rossa	$12,800
1964 250GT	$12,900
1965 330GT 2+2	$14,200
1967 330GTS	$14,200
1970 Dino 246 GTS	$14,500

Source: ferrarichat.com

In 2018, David MacNeil, WeatherTech's CEO and founder, paid $70 million for a car like those Mr. Merritt snubbed. Thus, Mr. MacNeil's Tour-de-France winning Ferrari 250 GTO (1962 list price $18,000) became the most expensive automobile ever sold. Until 2022. In a low-profile auction by its manufacturer, an ultra-rare 1955 Mercedes-Benz 300 SLR Uhlenhaut Coupé went for $143 million to a London broker bidding for an unnamed client. Only two such cars were ever made. Based on the W196 Grand Prix car which won two World Championships for driver Juan

Manual Fangio, the more powerful Uhlenhaut Coupés never saw competition—a disastrous accident at Le Mans in 1955 caused the Stuttgart firm to withdraw from racing.

"Frankly, a single high-dollar sale from the manufacturer's private collection has little or no impact on the general market," commented John Kraman, a Mecum Auctions spokesman. Still, he added, "prices across the board are extraordinarily high right now." Mecum scored a record-setting $126.5 million at its nine-day Indy 2022 auction during the same month the Mercedes changed hands.

MOST EXPENSIVE CARS EVER SOLD AT PUBLIC AUCTION: A SAMPLING

1957 FERRARI 335 SPORT SCAGLIETTI

$35.7M

Auctioneers at Artcurial Motorcar's 2016 Retromobile sale in Paris compared this car to paintings by Picasso and sculptures by Rodin. One of only four models made, the 335 S was equipped with a brutish, nearly 400-horsepower V-12 engine capable of propelling it to a then-remarkable speed of 190 miles per hour. Its extensive racing history included being piloted by legendary drivers such as Mike Hawthorn and Sir Stirling Moss. Tragically, the car was involved in a crash at the 1957 Mille Miglia that claimed a dozen lives and led to the race's cancellation (it continues today as a classic car rally). For a time—until two years later, when a 250 GTO crossed the auction block for $44 million—the 335 S reigned as the most expensive car ever publicly sold.

1954 MERCEDES-BENZ W196

$29.7M

It would be difficult to imagine a car with a more storied combination of rarity and distinguished racing history than the 2.5-liter, straight-eight Grand Prix racer that put Stuttgart back on top in international competition. Mercedes built only sixteen Silver Arrow cars and at the time of its sale at Bonhams' Goodwood auction in 2013, only ten remained extant. After the factory converted the formerly enclosed *Stromlinienwagen* to an open-wheel version, racing legend Juan Manuel Fangio won both the German and the Swiss Grands Prix, the latter win clinching his second World Championship (he eventually captured the title five times). An official certificate from Mercedes Benz confirmed that the car purchased was indeed chassis 00006, the Formula 1 car driven by the Argentinian at the German and Swiss events.

1956 FERRARI 290 MM

$28M

After Mercedes withdrew from racing following the 1955 Le Mans disaster, which claimed the lives of eighty-three spectators, Ferrari resolved to capture the World Sportscar Championship. One of only four models built, the 290 MM featured a 3.5-liter V-12 engine designed by the legendary engineer Vittorio Jano and specifically tailored to the specifications of Juan Manuel Fangio. The shorter, wider block was fitted with two spark plugs per cylinder, improving combustion and raising horsepower. Fangio raced the speedy barchetta (essentially a fully-fendered open car with a small windshield) in the 1956 Mille Miglia. Despite torrential rain, a last-place starting position, and no copilot to call out turns and hazards, the man many call the greatest race car driver of all time came in fourth among nearly five hundred cars that began the 1,000-mile event. Later notable drivers would include Phil Hill, Peter Collins, and Wolfgang von Trips, among others.

1967 FERRARI 275 GTB/4 S NART SPIDER

$27.5M

Originally priced at $15,000, the 275 GTB/4 is one of only ten NART (North American Racing Team) Spiders ever produced. The car boasted a 300-horsepower V-12 engine with four camshafts and, when sold by RM Auctions (now RM Sotheby's) in 2014, chassis 10709 had had a single owner who took possession directly from the Ferrari production line in 1967. Variously owned (and crashed) by Steve McQueen and pursued by Ralph Lauren, the Scaglietti roadster was called "the most satisfying sports car in the world" by Road & Track magazine. The car boasted a 300-horsepower, V-12 engine with six Weber carburetors and a five-speed gearbox. Featured in the McQueen film The Thomas Crown Affair, the 275 was originally purchased in 1968 by Eddie Smith, a self-made millionaire who had been orphaned as a child. Upon his death, Mr. Smith's family decided to donate the proceeds from the NART sale to charities, including the orphanage where he once lived. This car also briefly ranked as both the highest priced Ferrari and the most expensive road car ever publicly sold.

1956 ASTON MARTIN DBR1

$22.5M

One of only five models ever built and the first ever to change hands publicly, this DBR1 became the most expensive British car ever sold at auction when the hammer fell at RM Sotheby's during Monterey Car Week in 2017. Often called "the most important Aston Martin ever produced," the DBR1 was designed to race at Le Mans, an event it never won. Nonetheless, the "green machine" gave Stirling Moss one of his greatest come-from-behind triumphs. Rejected by Enzo Ferrari early in his career, Moss harbored a deep dislike for the Prancing Horse racers. At the 1,000-kilometer Nürburgring race in 1959, he led early on before yielding to his relief driver, who promptly drove off the road. Taking the wheel two more times, Moss refused to give up, posting screaming laps that regained the lead. He finally crossed the finish line first and less than a minute ahead of Phil Hill . . . in a Ferrari. During its racing lifetime, the DBR1 was driven by other well-known drivers, including Carroll Shelby and Jack Brabham. The DBR1's I-6 engine evolved from its debut in 1956 through its last race in 1959, ending up at 2,992 cc and 268 horsepower. In 2001, the car received the "Most Elegant Sports Car" trophy at the Pebble Beach Concours d'Elegance.

1955 JAGUAR D-TYPE

$21.8M

In 2016, RM Sotheby's auctioned a 1955 Jaguar D-Type for $21.8 million, thereby selling one of the most important Jaguars ever produced. Still in original condition as raced to victory at Le Mans in 1954 by Ecurie Ecosse, it had had only a pair of private owners since that race. At Le Mans, sometimes cited as the most grueling contest in sports car racing, the D-Type averaged 104 mph, reaching a peak of 156 mph on the famous Mulsanne straight. A Sotheby's specialist touted the car as the most original Le Mans winner from the 1950s. The car featured a 3.4-liter, six-cylinder engine making 250 horsepower and four-wheel, Jaguar-pioneered Dunlop disc brakes. Jaguar built just seventeen works D-Type racers, which earned three straight Le Mans victories from 1955 to 1957. By comparison, at its 2021 auction in Scottsdale, Arizona, Sotheby's sold a 1955 D Jag, without Le Mans history and painted an almost-Ferrari red rather than British racing green, for a mere $6 million.

1994 MCLAREN F1 "LM SPECIFICATION"

$19.8M

One of only two F1's modified to mimic the car that won the 24-hour Le Mans, this road-capable version included a 684-horsepower V-12 racing engine, modified steering and exhaust systems, 18-inch wheels, and the firm's Extra-High Downforce Package. The result of a twenty-four-month factory project and expected to bring $23 million at RM Sotheby's Monterey Car Week auction in 2019, the gray three-seater still managed to set a world record for the marque at auction.

1939 ALFA ROMEO 8C 2900B LUNGO SPIDER

$19.8M

The purchase of a 1930s Alfa Romeo 2900 8C, sometimes described as the prewar equivalent of a Ferrari 250 GTO, gained entry for its buyer to a very select fraternity. Acknowledged as one of the most beautiful cars ever made, only a dozen Lungo (Long) Spiders were in existence when this model was offered by RM Sotheby's in 2016. Equipped with a Vittorio Jano–designed straight-eight engine that boasted two superchargers, the car was graced by Touring's jaw-dropping Superleggera tube-and-alloy coachwork. Like many cars of its day, this model was rebodied and re-engined (with a Chevrolet V-8!) during the 1950s for racing purposes in South America. In the 1990s, it was reunited with its original body, chassis, and drivetrain and a full restoration carried out under the watchful eyes of then-owners and well-known collectors Sam and Emily Mann.

1961 FERRARI 250 GT SWB CALIFORNIA SPIDER

$18.5M

"In 1961," stated RM Sotheby's sales description, "a gentleman driver could drive his California Spider to the racetrack, easily outrun comparable Aston Martins and Jaguars, and drive home again in the early evening with the top down and in utmost comfort." The car's dual-purpose nature appealed to many well-heeled individuals, and SWB California Spiders were owned by film stars, such as Alain Delon, James Coburn, and Roger Vadim; European aristocracy, including Vittorio Emanuele of Savoy; and even racing drivers. Jan de Vroom campaigned his SWB California Spider at both the 1960 24-hour Le Mans and the 1961 12-hour Sebring, where he finished twelfth overall, an incredible result for a street-legal convertible. One of just sixteen open-headlight short wheelbase California Spiders, this car was fully restored by Ferrari Classiche. It featured a 3.0-liter V-12 engine with three Weber carburetors, disc brakes at all corners, and a four-speed manual transmission. Ownership of a California Spider, the catalog copy continued, "is something that almost every Ferrari enthusiast aspires to yet something that few can attain. It is the epitome of la dolce vita in the automotive world, as it combines timeless style with incredible performance." Chassis 2505GT was sold on the shores of Lake Como in March 2015.

The aforementioned SSJ Duesenberg owned by Gary Cooper was valued at $5,000 when acquired new by the actor. At the time of its 2018 auction, however, predictions were that Cooper's two-seater would fetch $10 million. Instead, the car hammered at $22 million, more than 200 percent higher. Even more-common collectibles are making impressive leaps. A 1956 Chevrolet Corvette that cost $3,308 when new is currently valued at nearly $80,000 in "No. 2" condition, according to Hagerty.

It should be noted that, with the exception of Mr. MacNeil's 250 GTO, all the sales cited were achieved at public auctions. So-called "private treaty" transactions, often the result of collectors pursuing a given car for years or even decades, can be much higher. What common attributes are shared by cars of such staggering value? First, all the models mentioned exist in extremely small quantities. In other words, like works of fine art, they are rare. Significantly, none of the models in our sampling of the most expensive cars was produced in more than two digits. Even the highest production European car cited, the Lancia Aurelia Spider, achieved a total run of just 240 units between 1954 and 1955. By comparison, more than 3,600 Chevrolet Corvettes were manufactured in 1956 alone. Is it surprising, then, that in 2014, Gooding & Company auctioned an Aurelia Spider for $1.8 million?

Just how rare are the highest valued classics? In the nearly four decades between 1947 (when the newly launched firm made just two cars) and 1984, Ferrari only produced about 10,000 automobiles, observed Bruce Trenery of Fantasy Junction, a global dealer in vintage vehicles for the past five decades. That works out to less than 300 units a year. Contrast the Italian automaker's output with that of Chevrolet. During those same thirty-seven years, GM produced and sold more than 100 *million* (101,266,018 to be exact) Chevy-branded cars and trucks—*10,000 times as many vehicles as Ferrari.*

Meanwhile, during the same period that European car production was creeping ahead by inches, the world's postwar population of potential classic car buyers boomed. In 1947, the year the 126 S—Ferrari's first badged car—rolled onto Via Abetone Inferiore in Maranello, Henry Ford died. That left H. L. Hunt as the world's only billionaire. Today, nearly 3,000 billionaires trod the planet, with a total net worth of more than $13 trillion. "A new billionaire was minted every seventeen hours on average over the past year," reported Forbes in 2021.

The growth in millionaires has been even more dramatic. Various estimates put the number of U.S. millionaires at around 5,000 in 1900. By 2021, nearly 20 million American households held more than $1 million in assets excluding their primary residences. Meanwhile, according to the Boston Consulting Group, in the past two decades alone, the number of global millionaires tripled.

"We've reached a point," said Mr. Trenery, "where there are just a lot more buyers than there are collectible cars." Of course, factors other than sheer numerical rarity factor into the value of cars. Possessing a distinguished history ranks high among them. A 1950 Cisitalia-Abarth driven by the legendary Tazio Nuvolari

Bruce Trenery of Fantasy Junction

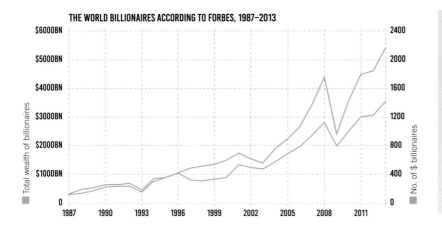

THE WORLD BILLIONAIRES ACCORDING TO FORBES, 1987–2013

Between 1987 and 2013, the number of billionaires rose according to Forbes, from 140 to 1400, and their total wealth climbed from 300 to 5,400 billion dollars.

in his last race is more valuable than the same car driven by Bernard Schwartz. Indeed, "provenance"—a car's origins and history—is a key component of value, whether the vehicle in question is an ultra rare racing Cisitalia, Gary Cooper's Duesenberg roadster, or a modern Honda NSX.

Another consideration that can add to a given car's value is the degree to which it has been "coachbuilt"—that is, built by hand. As we shall see in the following chapter, by the close of the 1960s many of the European coachbuilders like Touring, Ghia, and Vignale had ceased operation. Those coachbuilt cars also tended to be made in small numbers; only 2,200 Touring-bodied Alfa Romeo 2600 Spiders were manufactured between 1962 and 1965, for example. Other coachbuilt production runs were even smaller. By the 1980s, Mr. Trenery's Fantasy Junction firm was running newspaper ads urging potential buyers to "drive an investment." In point of fact, collectible cars, not unlike works of art, became an alternative to traditional holdings in stocks, bonds, and real estate. In the decade preceding 2019, classic car values rose by 194 percent, according to the Knight Frank Luxury Investment Index. (The only category outperforming collectible automobiles was rare whiskey.) Even in 2020,

the first year of the global pandemic, collectible car values held up.

If you're buying a classic car in hopes of turning a fast buck, however, think again. Like all assets, vintage automobiles can go down as well as up. In fact, those same 1980s that began with heady increases in collector car prices ended in a several-years slump. The price behavior of the Ferrari 275 GTB/4 offers a compelling example. At the beginning of 1987, the car *MotorTrend Classic* ranked third on its list of the ten best Ferraris of all time could be had for as little as $80,000. With the "Black Monday" stock market crash on October 19 that year, however, millions of panicked investors dumped their stocks and bonds and poured money into so-called "hard" assets—like real estate, precious metals, and classic cars. The result: By the end of 1989, the going price for a 275 GTB/4 had risen to $1.2 million. In fact, one prominent restorer turned down such money and more before collector cars experienced a collapse of their own. In the early 1990s, the same owner was forced to sell his GTB/4 for $700,000 less when he needed funds to purchase a home. It would take nearly twenty years for GTB/4 values to again reach their previous heights. In another example, an ambitious Stanford MBA raised $2 million from

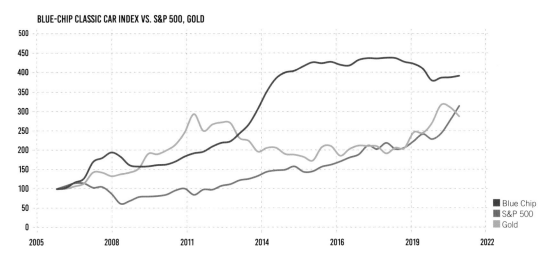

BLUE-CHIP CLASSIC CAR INDEX VS. S&P 500, GOLD

■ Blue Chip
■ S&P 500
■ Gold

Note: *Hagerty*'s Blue Chip index spans a diverse group of twenty-five cars deemed rare, expensive, and possessing wide global appeal. The list: 1967 Chevrolet Corvette; 1957 Mercedes 300 SL Gullwing; 1966 Shelby Cobra 427 (3300–3360); 1965 Shelby GT 350; 1969 Toyota 2000GT; 1959 Maserati 5000 GT Frua; 1958 Ferrari 250 California LWB; 1954 Lancia Aurelia B24; 1972 Iso Grifo Can Am; 1970 Plymouth Barracuda; 1958 Bentley Continental S1; 1964 Alfa Romeo TZ-2; 1963 MBZ 300 SL Roadster; 1953 Chevrolet Corvette; 1965 Aston Martin DB5; 1948 Tucker 48; 1973 Porsche 911 Carrera RS 2.7; 1963 Shelby Cobra 289 R&P; 1954 Jaguar D; 1958 Porsche 356A 1600 Super; 1963 Ferrari 250 California SWB; 1957 Rolls-Royce Mulliner Silver Cloud; 1968 Ferrari 275 GTB/4; 1959 BMW 507; 1971 Lamborghini Miura P400 SV.

ten enthusiast-investors, hoping to create a fund for the purchase of collectible cars, which could also be pleasure-driven on a rotating basis. "Ten years later he would have reaped multiple returns," said Mr. Trenery, "but he wound up having to unload the cars at a loss after prices collapsed."

Even so, through ups and downs, classic cars have been mostly kind to investors. Using 2006–2021 data, Hagerty, the Traverse, Michigan, firm that insures and tracks the value of collector automobiles and specialty vehicles, compared the performance of classic cars with so-called traditional investments. Seen on the next page, the results reflect updated *Hagerty Price Guide* values based on data collected via public auctions, car dealer sales, "private treaty" transactions reported by members, and asking prices displayed on internet sites. As can be seen, blue-chip collector cars outpaced stocks over the past fifteen years, gaining an impressive 292 percent versus the S&P 500's

214 percent and also outpacing the price of gold over the same period. (Hagerty statistics separately show that "affordable" classics also grew in value, though they lagged the S&P; the firm's "Hagerty 100," which tracks the values of the most common postwar collectible cars and trucks, remained unchanged.)

At least as impressive has been the resilience demonstrated by classic cars when downturns did occur. Following the 1990s slump, collectible vehicles weathered both the early 2000s' dot-com bust and the Great Recession of 2008–2010. In an in-depth look at the latter period, Hagerty concluded that, although initial values did drop, prices of blue-chip, low-production classics bottomed out within twenty-four months and fully recovered after three years. Garden-variety classics were slower to come back, Hagerty found. By mid-2012, however, nearly all cars were on a solid trajectory to future increases in value. And in 2014, collector car prices reached a still unequaled pinnacle.

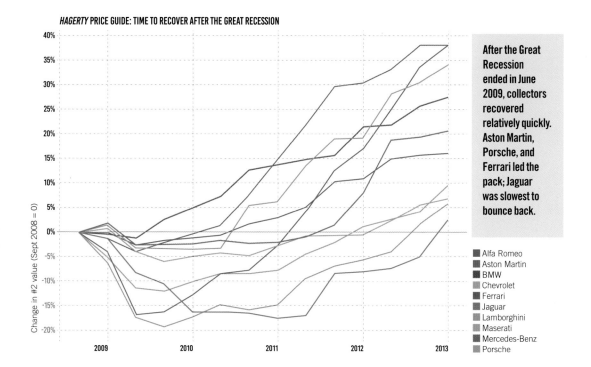

HAGERTY PRICE GUIDE: TIME TO RECOVER AFTER THE GREAT RECESSION

Change in #2 value (Sept 2008 = 0)

After the Great Recession ended in June 2009, collectors recovered relatively quickly. Aston Martin, Porsche, and Ferrari led the pack; Jaguar was slowest to bounce back.

- Alfa Romeo
- Aston Martin
- BMW
- Chevrolet
- Ferrari
- Jaguar
- Lamborghini
- Maserati
- Mercedes-Benz
- Porsche

Six years later, however, collector car values faced a critical test. As the result of the 2020s' global pandemic, automobile events all over the world were abruptly canceled, with devastating effects on live auctions, municipal tax revenues, concours d'elegance, and showrooms like Mr. Trenery's, where foot traffic dropped by more than 90 percent. More than twenty scheduled events—annually attended by thousands of enthusiasts—were called off during Monterey, California's Car Week alone. In addition to the Pebble Beach Concours d'Elegance, they included five major auctions, separate large-scale shows for Italian and German vehicles, and many other auto-oriented gatherings and events. The week's North America–leading auction sales—which in the nine years since 2010 had grossed some $3 billion—vanished like clouds of vapor from a Stanley Steamer. Charities saw millions in donations disappear.

Despite the damage, however, sales of collectible cars continued and, in some cases, thrived. Many brick-and-mortar dealers, Fantasy Junction among them, ramped up their internet listings. Others launched their own online auctions and worked their global networks of collectors. As David Gooding, president of Gooding & Company, told the *New York Times*, "2020 was rough—the whole live auction industry was down." His firm, based in Santa Monica, California, grossed some $125 million, well below its best years. "But we feel grateful for what we still managed to accomplish and for what we learned," he said. For example, the pandemic prompted the company to hasten its introduction of Geared Online, a web platform featuring both vintage cars and automotive memorabilia.

Though few in number, the live auctions in 2020 often posted impressive results. During a brief window when such gatherings could be held in the United Kingdom, Mr. Gooding's firm managed to stage a live "Passions of a Lifetime" sale at London's historic Hampton Court. Featuring fifteen superlative classics, the one-day event's proceeds topped $44 million and

achieved a 93 percent sell-through rate. It also boasted a towering average price per car of $3.1 million and the highest amount ever publicly paid for a classic Bugatti—$12.7 million for a 1934 Type 59 Sports. The Bugatti also scored the year's high for a publicly sold collector car, the company said.

Despite being scattered, other events during the year were similarly successful. In July 2020, proceeds topped $74 million at Mecum's Indianapolis auction, results that included $3.85 million, the top price ever paid for a Mustang. The auctioneer billed the car, a 1965 Shelby Mustang GT350R prototype once driven by racer Ken Miles (portrayed in the movie *Ford v Ferrari*), as "the most important in the history of the marque." Three months later, it took RM Sotheby's a scant five minutes to auction three of Alfa Romeo's famous B.A.T. cars for $14 million-plus at a live virtual-sale in New York.

Founded in 1909, Bugatti was a maker of sports, racing, and luxury automobiles. The Type 59 was the firm's final race car of the 1930s. A Type 59 sold for $9.5 million at Gooding & Co.'s "Passion of a Lifetime" auction in London during the 2020 Pandemic—the highest hammer price achieved by a single car that year.

Perhaps most impressive, however, were the results achieved by Bring-a-Trailer.com, an increasingly popular website for buying and selling vintage automobiles. Already coming off a torrid 2019, when its sales reached an all-time high of some $240 million, the site experienced a gold rush in 2020, climbing more than 60 percent to $398 million. For the year, BaT sold nearly a thousand cars a month. "Nobody knew what would happen in March or April," Randy Nonnenberg, the firm's cofounder and president, told the *New York Times*, "but many [more] people tasted and tested what it

1931 Cadillac V-16 Seven-Passenger Imperial Sedan. Cadillac built slightly more than 4,000 V-16 automobiles during an 11-year run, more than half in 1930 before the full impact of the Great Depression. The cars ranged in various models from the Imperial Sedan to a Dual Cowl Sports Phaeton. The Classic Car Club of America ranks the V-16s as among the finest vehicles built from 1925–1948. The car above sold for $72,800 at RM Sothebys Scottsdale, AZ, auction in 2020.

was like to transact online in a socially restricted environment. They now see this as a useful and effective way to pursue their interests, including collectible cars."

Human emotion played a critical role in such decisions. Facing a frightening pandemic, along with ongoing political and economic turmoil, many potential collectible car buyers decided the time had come to seize their dreams. That attitude continued to fuel sales as 2021 began, with Mecum Auctions scoring a record $122.8 million at its annual Kissimmee, Florida, event in January. Despite strict social distancing rules, live, online, and phone bidders competed for more than three thousand vintage vehicles over the ten-day auction. At a separate, single-day sale later that month, RM Sotheby's took in $35 million in Scottsdale, Arizona.

Any serious discussion of classic automobiles as an investment, however, must confront a factor that seldom impacts more traditional assets such as stocks, bonds, or real estate—changing generational tastes.

The kinds of automobiles that made our sample list of expensive sales in the second decade of the 2000s are vastly different than they might have been in the 1970s or '80s. The reader will find no Cadillac V-16 Sport Phaetons, Dual-Cowl Packard Lebarons, Cord 812s, or custom Graham Hollywood sedans among them. While many of those venerable machines still command prices well into six figures, they rarely reach the stratospheric heights of marques like Lamborghini, McLaren, Ferrari and rare Alfa Romeos—or even sought-after American performance cars such as the first Shelby Cobra, which sold for $13.75 million in 2016.

As Mark J. McCourt noted in a May 2021 article for *Hemmings Classic Car*, the vehicles "we find ourselves most drawn to—perhaps those that populated the roads when we were impressionable children, or those we aspired to when we came of driving age—get older along with us." Based on searches for automobile insurance and value data, baby boomers (those born between 1946 and 1964) still dominate the rarefied turf occupied by $10 million-plus cars, according to Hagerty. Coming up fast behind them, however, are well-heeled millennials whose presence can only be expected to grow over time.

The coming force of NextGen purchasing power can already be seen in the steady uptick in values of previously ignored Japanese models, American cars like Fox-bodied Ford Mustangs, and even some newish and/or neglected European models. For example, the Porsche 911 SC, made from 1978 to 1983, for years languished in the $10,000 to $12,000 range. More recently, a model in good condition—the SC's sturdy (and speedy) flat-six aluminum engine can manage 200,000 miles before needing a major overhaul—can fetch around $50,000.

So, what's the best course of action for those new to the hobby? The author suggests they heed Mr. Trenery's sage advice: "Buy what you love, and buy the best you can." We'll have more to say about that later.

4

NEXTGEN
WOMEN

"Dona e Motori, Gioi e Dolori— Women and Motors, Joy and Pain."

Motto painted on Tazio Nuvolari's racing Alfa Romeo

S he was young, beautiful, rich, and—as the title of her biography suggests— *Indomita*[1]. Friend of writer Ernest Hemingway, painter Amedeo Modigliani, actress Anna Magnani, and poet Gabriele D'Annunzio, she was also, for a time at least, auntie-in-law of Ingrid (Rossellini) Bergman. Most notably, memorably, and gloriously, however, she was fast. As the first woman in the world to appear in the Targa Florio (1920), the Mille Miglia (1928), and at Indianapolis (1932), she was Italy's most famous female race car driver.

Meet Baroness Maria Antonietta Avanzo. She, who Enzo Ferrari described as having driven with "confidence and precision" in winning her class at the Giro del Lazio in 1920. She, who shared a third-in-class finish with her teammate—none other than the legendary Tazio

Among Baroness Avanzo's motorsports contemporaries were Enzo Ferrari, founder of the Ferrari marque, and, pictured, Tazio Nuvolari, ranked among the greatest race car drivers of all time. In the 1920s, Nuvolari team-raced with Avanzo; in 1935, in a smaller Alfa Romeo, she defeated Nazi Germany's most powerful Mercedes and Auto Union racers at the Nurburgring Grand Prix.

Nuvolari—at the Circuito di Garda in 1921. She, who, beginning in 1928, entered the Mille Miglia five times, driving such machines as an Alfa Romeo 6C 1759 SS, a Bugatti T43, and a Scuderia Ferrari Alfa provided by her friend Enzo. And finally, she, who—at a time when the Speedway forbade women participants—was invited by Ralph DePalma, lifetime winner of some 2,000 races, to drive his Miller Special in an exhibition at the Indy 500 in 1932.

On at least two occasions, Baroness Avanzo raced against Ferrari himself: at Targa Florio in 1922, where she was forced to withdraw in the second lap, and at Circuito di Garda in

[1] *Indomita, la straordinaria vita di Maria Antonietta Avanzo*, by Luca Malin, 2013.

1927, where "il Commendatore" finished fifth and Baroness Avanzo came in tenth. "Today, a woman can easily drive with the same safety and ability as a man," Avanzo told the writer Gigliola Gori in 1928. "Does a woman driver lose her aesthetic femininity? On the contrary, I suggest that her elegant figure perfectly suits the line of a car and that they complement each other."

The baroness retired in 1939 following a sixth-place finish at Tobruk-Tripoli, which had temporarily supplanted the then suspended Mille Miglia. She was fifty. "She spent her life fighting prejudice, ostracism, obstacles, and men," observed her biographer Luca Malin, "especially when they would throw things in her way or herd sheep onto the track to stop her from getting to the finish line" (which caused her Targa Floria withdrawal). Avanzo herself had no regrets. "I've done everything that I ever wanted to do," she said. "I've been very blessed: beauty, wealth, great loves, and two splendid children . . . and if the car went to 180 miles per hour, I went at 180 miles per hour." She died in Italy in 1977 at age eighty-seven.

Eleven years after the demise of the woman *Italian Ways* magazine called the "Queen of Motors," Tabetha Hammer was born on a farm in Pueblo, Colorado. "I grew up working with my hands—it's part of who I am," said Ms. Hammer, now president and CEO of Tacoma, Washington–based America's Automotive Trust. AAT supports organizations such as LeMay – America's Car Museum; LeMay-affiliate the RPM Foundation, which funds automotive preservation and restoration education; and Allentown, Pennsylvania–based America on Wheels Museum. The trust's goal: "To honor and expand America's automotive heritage."

It would be hard to imagine anyone more suited for that role than the millennial Ms. Hammer. As a high school student, she restored a 1935 John Deere Model B tractor that her grandfather had purchased from its elderly first owner, a local rancher. The deal included a bag of original parts. "I didn't go on dates or see any movies that summer," recalled Hammer, who figured she put in more than 200 hours on the project. Her efforts paid off when she became the first female to win an annual nationwide tractor restoration competition sponsored by Chevron and the Future Farmers of America.

Her successful tractor project led to acceptance at McPherson College, a Kansas college that offers degrees in automotive restoration; the school says two-thirds of its students land jobs before they graduate, three times the national average. Ms. Hammer received training in paint and bodywork, and mechanical, chassis, and interior refurbishment while pursuing a concentration in automotive communications. Prior to her AAT post, she oversaw Hagerty's youth and education initiatives and served as director of the Greenwich Concours d'Elegance.

Ms. Hammer says women today are playing significant roles in all aspects of the hobby, from vintage motorsports to collecting. "Trust me," she insists, "there are a lot of young women out there who love cars." She herself drives a vintage Austin Mini and at the time of this writing was actively looking for a race car.

One woman who's found her ride is Gracie Hackenberg. As a mechanical engineering student at Smith College in Northampton, Massachusetts, Ms. Hackenberg gained national attention by converting a rust bucket 1999 Mazda Miata into a full-blown race car. Armed with a welding torch, a GoFundMe account, a college engineering grant, and help from as many as forty eager Smith students, she fitted the vehicle with a roll cage, new exhaust system, racing seat, safety harness, and spoiler. Entering Florida's 2017 Grassroots Motorsports Challenge (which limited entrants' preparation costs to just $2,017), Ms. Hackenberg and her team earned a respectable seventh-place finish and feature coverage in *The Wall Street Journal*, *Autoweek*, and other national media.

TABETHA HAMMER
Shown wrenching Hagerty's 1969 "Comeback Camaro SS," she's currently president and CEO of Tacoma, Washington–based America's Automotive Trust.

Ms. Hackenberg also caught the attention of the RPM Foundation, an arm of Ms. Hammer's AAT, which supports training programs for NextGen automotive restorers and preservationists. That led to introductions to mentors such as famed woman racer Lyn St. James (more about her later) and Brian Donovan, whose shop in Lennox, Massachusetts, is known for rebuilding and racing vintage European cars. After graduation in 2018, she joined the firm as a full-time employee and two years later earned her Sports Car Club of America racing license. She's currently training as a mechanic at Arrow McLaren SP, an Indianapolis-based firm that competes in the Indianapolis 500 and NTT IndyCar Series races.

Just how unique are women like Maria Antonietta Avanzo, Tabetha Hammer, and Gracie Hackenberg? Not as unusual as you might think. A nonexhaustive list compiled by author Jean-François Bouzanquet in his exhaustive 2017 work, *Fast Ladies: Female Racing Drivers 1888 to 1970*, counted no fewer than 565 women who played important—if often underrecognized—roles as motorsports and automotive enthusiasts during those eighty-two years. Each made an important contribution to the acceptance of females in auto racing, later as a presence in the world of collecting and, ultimately, as a powerful force for recognizing cars as objects d'art.

Among the earliest was Bertha Benz, wife of Carl Benz, widely hailed as the inventor of the world's first practical automobile in 1886. Achieving recognition in the press, however, had proven ephemeral for Mr. Benz, a technically gifted engine designer and engineer. His groundbreaking new gasoline-powered car failed to generate enthusiasm among the public, which generally dismissed the vehicle as unsuitable for practical use. Carl Benz's business associates started turning away and Benz himself began to lose confidence in the project. Bertha, however, had staunchly supported her husband from the beginning; she quickly grasped the significance of his invention—the only missing element was

proof that the vehicle could safely traverse long distances.

In the dark of night on August 5, 1888, after leaving a note for still-sleeping Carl, Bertha quietly crept with the couple's two teenage sons—still on summer vacation—to the Benz workshop. Together, the trio pushed the bulky Motorwagen until it was safely away from the house. Then, after they'd given the massive

BERTHA BENZ
The wife of the producer of the world's first gasoline-powered automobile is shown at the wheel of the Benz Velo, the firm's first production car—1,200 were made from 1894–1900.

flywheel a few swings back and forth, the engine *fumph-fumph-fumphed* to life. Thus began an historic 111-mile journey from Mannheim to Mrs. Benz's mother's home in Pforzheim and back again—the first long-distance trip by an automobile.

Along the way, Bertha and her boys, ages fourteen and fifteen, were frequently forced to jump out and push the car; it lacked the necessary gearing to climb hills. She stopped at a local cobbler to have the brake shoes covered with leather (thus inventing the first brake linings); procured ligroine (petroleum ether) from a pharmacy to refill the meager 4.5-liter tank; cleared a blocked fuel line with her hatpin; and, in what Bouzanquet describes as "the height of eroticism," insulated the car's worn ignition cable with one of her garters.

ALICE HUYLER RAMSEY
Ignoring their long dresses, hats and dusters, Alice and her female friends drove a new Maxwell across country. Occasionally the trip meant fixing a flat tire or an unscheduled encounter with surprised (but not unfriendly) Native Americans.

Mrs. Benz's epic journey was worth the effort. Besides silencing the critics and shoring up her husband's spirits, she'd attracted worldwide attention. She'd proved that an automobile could safely complete a long trip and she'd also demonstrated the utility of test-drives—Bertha's car was given a third gear and a vastly improved brake as a direct result of her experience. By 1894, the fledgling Benz company had produced twenty-five cars, with engines ranging from 1.5 to 3 horsepower.

Two decades later in America, women would match Mrs. Benz's feat. On June 9, 1909, a twenty-two-year-old Vassar graduate named Alice Huyler Ramsey took the wheel of a new, 30-horsepower Maxwell DA and, after posing for photographers in New York City, set off with three female passengers on a 3,800-mile trip to San Francisco. It would be the longest automobile trip ever undertaken by an American woman.

The background: After watching Ms. Ramsey drive her own Maxwell impressively in a local rally, Maxwell executives offered to give her a new car and pay all her expenses if she'd agree to drive across the country as a publicity stunt. Accompanying her were two sisters-in-law in their forties and a sixteen-year-old girl friend. Like Ms. Ramsey herself, who was married to a successful politician (who did not drive), all three women were from upper-class backgrounds. As such, they set off in hats, gloves, and dusters to protect their long dresses; Ms. Ramsey, the only one among them who possessed a license, wore a driving helmet and goggles to shield herself from the dust, mud, and rain that surged over the car's low windshield. Besides hand-cranking the vehicle

to start it, checking the fuel level required lifting out the front seat and dipping a ruler into the 20-gallon tank. During their arduous journey, the women repaired eleven flat tires, refilled the car's steam-spouting radiator with river water, and lashed the suspension together with bailing wire. At the time, the entire U.S. highway system consisted of fewer than 200 miles of paved roadway; after crossing the Mississippi River, most of the country was unmapped. The women followed telephone wires to towns and cities. Traveling west, they encountered new challenges. Sleeping beside campfires, they shivered to the sound of howling coyotes; in Nevada, they startled—and were startled by—a group of Native Americans on horseback with drawn bows and arrows, but the tribesmen were only hunting rabbits.

On August 7, 1909, the women reached San Francisco, having traveled for fifty-nine days—three weeks longer than planned. "Pretty Women Motorists Arrive after Trip Across the Continent" one headline read. For Alice Ramsey, motoring was in her blood. Between 1909 and 1975, she would drive across the country more than two dozen times.

Driving at speed, however, was another matter. Although European women like Baroness Avanzo figured prominently in motorsports, most American women would not follow suit, let alone emulate Alice Ramsey and put themselves behind the wheel on cross-country trips. A few early 1900s continental examples: France's aristocratic Camille du Gast, variously identified as the first or second woman to compete in an international race; Jeanne Herveaux, an incredible hillclimber on her Werner motorbike (and later pilot); and England's first female racing driver Dorothy Levitt, who after a starring turn in a publicity stunt, launched a racing career that included setting the women's world speed record in 1905.

As had the Baronesss Avanzo, however, Europe's greatest women of racing emerged in the 1920s and 1930s. Among them were Hellé Nice, aka "the Bugatti Queen," who set Grand Prix speed records; Odette Siko, who led an all-woman team including Nice in speed trials at Autodrome de Montlhéry, where they shattered twenty-five records, some of which still stand; and England's Jill Scott-Thomas, among the first women to be awarded Brookland Race Track's coveted 120-mile-per-hour badge and believed to be the first woman recommended for membership in the ultra-conservative British Automobile Racing Club (though accepted, her status was downgraded to honorary, unfortunately).

Before leaving the prewar continent, however, special mention must be made of Lucy O'Reilly Schell. Though a New Yorker, she was born in Paris and spent much of her life in Europe, racing cars. She became the first American woman to compete in an international Grand Prix and—in an achievement that would touch the pages of history—the first woman to establish her own Grand Prix team. The year was 1938 and the race was the Grand Prix de Pau in southwestern France. Hitler was determined his new 468-horsepower Mercedes Silver Arrow racers would continue Nazi dominance of motorsports. Instead, with half-Jewish René Dreyfus piloting a Delahaye 145 for Mrs. Schell's newly formed Écurie Bleue team, the Germans lost their only race in two years. The triumph, in the words of Motorsport.com writer William Cash, "reminded hundreds of thousands across Europe that no matter how improbable the odds seemed, victory against a seeming superior foe was always possible."

Europe's leadership of female auto racing faded after World War II, when a new breed of brash young American women fell in love with sporty foreign cars and the men who brought them back. The postwar vehicles from MG, Porsche, and Lancia were comparatively small, fitted with elegant leather and wood interiors, and amazingly easy to drive; they were also quick from the pedal, light in steering, and frugal at the gas pump. What wasn't to like (unless, of course, one was forced to hastily install side windows during a downpour)?

There were major exceptions to America's female racing leadership, of course, such as Pat Moss, sister of Stirling. The siblings' father had raced at Brooklands and Indianapolis and their mother had driven in rallies in the 1930s. Pat's motorsports career began in 1953 when her brother's manager asked her to serve as his navigator on a rally; for the next two decades, she collected wins across Europe, driving for Saab, Lancia, and other marques, often with her husband, Swedish rally champion Erik Carlsson. Other women, like Dutch driver and model Liane Engeman, also campaigned with success on the continent.

During the same period, however, American drivers like Evelyn Mull, Denise McCluggage,

and Ruth Levy were contesting SCCA events at Nassau, Sebring, Watkins Glen, and other racing venues in their respective AC Bristols, MGs, and Porsche 356s. Ms. Mull, who with her fellow-racer and husband, coal-mining heir John Mull, were members of Philadelphia's Main Line set, converted their horse trailers and stalls into car carriers and garage space. Across the mid-1950s, Evelyn—a better driver than John—collected wins against dozens of women and mixed competitors.

Journalist and race car driver Denise McCluggage shared a relationship with then unemployed actor Steve McQueen when both were struggling MGTC owners living in Manhattan. A trail-breaking sports journalist in a male-dominated universe, Ms. McCluggage lived life at speed, whether on ski slopes or racetracks. She competed at Nürburgring; won

JILL SCOTT
Heiress to a coal mining fortune, she was the first woman recommended for membership in the British Automobile Racing Club.

her class at Sebring in 1961, driving a Ferrari 250 GT; and captured classes at the Grand Prix of Venezuela and the Rallye Monte Carlo, driving, respectively, a Porsche 550 and a Ford Falcon in 1964. She became the only journalist ever awarded membership in the Automotive Hall of Fame.

Although Ruth Levy's accomplishments were overshadowed by those of McCluggage, she was another force to be reckoned with in the mid-1950s. A painter, cowboy poet, and occasional jazz singer, Ms. Levy started her career ice racing over the frozen lakes of Minnesota.

By 1957 she'd joined a Porsche team that included Carroll Shelby and campaigned across North and South America.

There were dozens of others, among them Maria Teresa de Filippis, who, in 1958, drove a Maserati 250F—the same car in which Fangio famously won at Nürburgring the year before—to become the first woman to qualify for a Formula One Grand Prix. Then, wrote Todd McCarthy in *Fast Women: The Legendary Ladies of Racing*, "suddenly and without their having seen it coming, it was over, sooner than seemed possible . . . not only did the women find a glass ceiling preventing their continuing up through the ranks, but there was glass all around them through which they could see their male friends and competitors continue doing what they all used to do together. The pressures of money, sponsorship, and the sport's shift to professionalism pushed them aside, and there was nowhere else for them to go."

Author McCarthy's gloomy descent notwithstanding, "it" did not end there, not all of it, and by no means forever. Certainly not for Janet Guthrie, who in 1977 became the first woman to qualify and compete in both the Indianapolis and Daytona 500. Nor for Lyn St. James, class winner at Daytona, Sebring, and Nürburgring; first woman to reach a track speed of more than 200 miles per hour (at Talladega in 1988); first female Rookie of the Year at the Indy 500 in 1992—and, at age forty-five, the oldest racer of either gender to be so recognized; first woman to win a sanctioned International

LIANE ENGEMAN
A top female Dutch driver in the 1960s, she drove for Ford and Auto Delta and was a multiple top five finisher in the European Touring Car Championships.

Motor Sports Association race driving solo (Watkins Glen, 1988); and, finally, named by *Sports Illustrated* as one of the "Top 100 Women Athletes of the Century" in 1996.

It also didn't end for Danica Patrick. And it didn't end for the late Sabine Schmitz, who became Nürburgring's most celebrated female racer ever. Known as the "queen" of those most beautiful and dangerous 14 miles, she carved her way through the "Green Hell" of the wooded Eifel mountains, flashing her wide white smile at cheering fans as she went. Overall winner of the 24-hour Nürburgring in 1996 and 1997 aboard her BMW 318iS, she drove Porsches to place finishes in the early 2000s. Icing her cake, she became a presenter on England's *Top Gear* television show. Sadly, the irrepressible Schmitz lost a long battle with cancer in 2021. She was only fifty-one.

After spending so much time on dusty roads and muddy racetracks, women today are finding a multitude of ways to express their love of swooping metal and roaring engines. Indeed, Footman James, a British collectible car insurance provider, reported in 2016 that the number of its female policyholders had increased by 40 percent in just two years. Across the pond, Akron, Ohio–based Anthony Thomas Advertising, a digital marketing firm, found that women aged eighteen to thirty-four made up 44 percent of automotive enthusiasts they surveyed.

Hagerty, the world's largest insurer of collector cars and specialty vehicles, offers a more conservative but still impressive—and updated—take on women's growing impact on the world of classic conveyances. According to the firm, its share of female policyholders grew from 8.2 to 10.6 percent between 2010 and

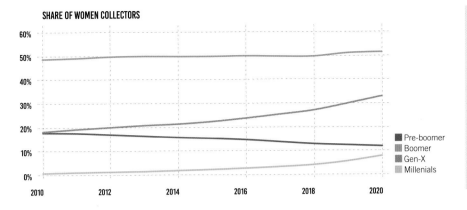

SHARE OF WOMEN COLLECTORS

Legend: Pre-boomer, Boomer, Gen-X, Millenials

Hagerty found that, though small in absolute numbers, female policyholders ensuring enthusiast vehicles grew by nearly a third between 2010 and 2020.

2020, still small numbers but an increase over the decade of more than 29 percent. Moreover, Hagerty noted, its figures cover only sole ownership by women and thus do not reflect the many collectible vehicles jointly owned with a husband or partner. As indicated by the chart above, the biggest increases were recorded by female members of Gen X (those born between 1965 and 1980) and millennials (those born between 1981 and 1996).

"The collectible car world has become far more diverse in recent years," said John Wiley, Hagerty's manager of valuation analytics. "At the same time, what constitutes an enthusiast vehicle has changed too. Thirty years ago serious collectors only bought prewar cars; twenty years ago they bought 1950s and '60s Ferrari; ten years ago they bought Porsches. Now collectible cars are more varied and so are their owners. Women collectors seem more focused on vintage vehicles they can actually use at 'cars and coffee' and other informal events."

Among the most ambitious surveys of female involvement with and enthusiasm for classic cars was undertaken in 2020 by *The Key*, the magazine of Liechtenstein-based the Classic Car Trust (TCCT). The survey covered 1,100 participants in the United States, England, Germany, Italy, France, and Switzerland. It included women "on the front line of participation," those who share the passion of husbands or partners, and "women drivers who do not have a relationship with the world of classic cars." The magazine concluded that its research demonstrated "that the female gender represents a formidable asset for the future . . . it would be unwise to underestimate their role as opinion leaders and potential stars."

Among its key findings:

Only 2 percent of women said they were "bored" at classic car events; more than 70 percent said they responded to classic cars emotionally, with "positive" feelings; more than 60 percent said they registered a sense of "joy" and/or "freedom."

Asked what kind of classic car they would use for leisure; 58 percent chose a 1950s–1960s sport model; next highest were 19 percent who opted for 1960s–1970s sports cars; only 1 percent preferred a prewar luxury automobile.

Sixty-seven percent said they attend car events to meet other people "with the same passion."

"The most requested item is to give the person in the passenger seat a real role in events," the TCCT surveyors reported, "especially when it comes to driving . . . young women, in particular, ask for gender equality."

One woman who needn't seek gender equality is Caroline Cassini, twenty-nine, already an accomplished collector, presenter, and purveyor of classic cars. With her father, retired New Jersey Superior Court Judge Joseph Cassini III and mother Margie, Caroline—who as a girl served as "chief washer, waxer, and professional cleaner" of the family car collection—shared in two Best of Show triumphs at Pebble Beach in 2004 and 2013. The starring cars, respectively: a 1938 Horch Sport Cabriolet and a 1934 Dietrich-bodied Packard Twelve Convertible.

"I've had incredible mentors," reflected Ms. Cassini. Among others, she cited her father; "second dad" Canada-based restorer and Sotheby's auction house partner Rob Myers; Bruce and Spencer Trenery of Fantasy Junction; well-known female collector Anne Brockinton Lee; and Lloyd Buck, her teacher at San Francisco's Academy of Art University, former manager of the famed Arturo Keller car collection, and current associate director of the academy's automotive restoration curriculum. Some of the critical skills and knowledge acquired by Ms. Cassini at SFAA: bronze casting, metal fabrication, paint and bodywork, and rejuvenation and repair of mechanical and electrical systems. Coming from Llewellyn Park, New Jersey, among America's most exclusive gated communities, Ms. Cassini admitted her choice to pursue what some might view as vocational training raised a few neighborhood eyebrows. "But if you have this passion, you can't care what others think," she said. "You must follow your dream."

CAROLINE CASSINI
Shown center stage at Bonhams 2022 auction in Scottsdale, Arizona, Cassini was named general manager of the firm's U.S. website.

After the academy, she went to work for Fantasy Junction, which responded to the 2020s pandemic by broadening its focus to selling cars online, often through the popular website Bring-a-Trailer.com. As it happened, however, her biggest thrill came with a car that failed to reach its BaT reserve, a 1934 Auburn Boat-Tail Speedster. "Prewar cars are my special love," explained Ms. Cassini, who worked her network and snagged a full-price offer of $850,000 from a collector in Florida. Ms. Cassini was recently named general manager of British-based Bonhams U.S. website, where she's pledged to include more listings aimed at NextGen buyers.

"Like Caroline, more and more young women want to participate," commented Theresa Gilpatrick, former longtime executive director of the Ferrari Club of America. As a tot, Ms. Gilpatrick remembers standing behind the wheel of her family's Chevrolet Bel-Air, and later saving her allowance for a Hot Wheels collection. Now in her fifties, she urges younger women to "go for it," whether their interest lies in car shows and collecting, motorsports, or all of the above. "Get on LinkedIn," she advised, "and search for women in the niche you're interested in. Reach out and don't be bashful. There's amazing support out there, you just have to tap into it."

S hortly before 8 p.m. EST, Cindy Sisson approaches her kitchen counter in Mooresville, North Carolina. Facing her is the notebook computer she will use to conduct a very special Zoom meeting. Pouring herself a cocktail, Ms. Sisson scans her notes. On the wall behind her is a photograph of the red Lola-Chevy race car Lyn St. James drove in 1992, when she became the first female named

as the Indy 500's Rookie of the Year. Painted across the ground-hugging, dart-shaped vehicle's front spoiler, and repeated atop its narrow fuselage, are the words, "Spirit of the American Woman."

Women Shifting Gears, a monthly, female-only virtual "Lap," is about to begin. For the next hour or two as many as 150 participants will hear remarks by a prominent automotive figure—Ms. St. James was the group's second speaker—then break into smaller online chat rooms to electronically mingle and kibbitz.

"At Women Shifting Gears, women occupy the driver's seat," says Ms. Sisson, CEO of GSEvents, which hosts the forums. The group can include journalists, vintage auto collectors, preservationists and restorers, club leaders, rally and race car drivers, and people, such as a member in Dubuque, Iowa, who just likes cars. "We even have one woman who owns a racetrack in Alaska," Sisson adds.

The group's original email invitation in late 2020 drew 200 replies; less than a year later, the Shifting Gears' platform includes 1,000 women. Typically gathering on the third Tuesday of every month, participants range in age

CINDY SISSON
"At Women Shifting Gears, women occupy the driver's seat," says Ms. Sisson, CEO of GSEvents, which hosts forums and events for female automotive enthusiasts. Here she's shown with history's winningest Ferrari, the fabled 1957 625/250 TRC Testa Rossa.

from fifteen to seventy-five, with the average hovering around thirty. "We have cocktails, share ideas about cars and jobs, and do a lot of connecting," Ms. Sisson notes. The Shifting Gears network brought one woman, automotive artist Lyn Hiner, an offer to display her work at the Saratoga Auto Museum in Saratoga Springs, New York. Other participants have landed jobs via the forum.

The group's guest speakers represent a who's who of women in the automotive space. Aside from Ms. St. James, they've included Beth Perretta, first female leader of a coed racing team at the Indianapolis 500 in 2021; Allyson Witherspoon, vice president and chief marketing officer at Nissan USA; Cindy Lucchese, chief strategy officer for racing icon Roger Penske–owned Penske Entertainment; and Amanda Busick, who covers National Hot

Rod Association events for Fox Sports and also produces and hosts a weekly Shifting Gears podcast. Among the show's early guests: Judy Stropus, legendary professional timer/scorer inducted into the Motorsports Hall of Fame in 2021.

"We're about empowering women," sums up Ms. Sisson. "Our main goal is to facilitate collaborative relationships that can help women grow in the automotive universe." With a background in youth sports and STEM (science, technology, engineering, and math) education, in addition to her role as GSEvents CEO, Ms. Sisson formerly served as a consultant to the TechForce Foundation, a group suggested by both Ms. Gilpatrick and Ms. Cassini as a potential pathway for young women interested in car-oriented careers. The Scottsdale, Arizona–based foundation offers scholarship support for restoration and other hands-on automotive fields. "We need to teach moms and dads that a technical profession is something they can be proud of," says Ms. Sisson, noting Ms. Cassini's focus on design and restoration at the San Francisco Academy of Art.

Another supportive voice comes from Sandra Button, longtime chair of the Pebble Beach Concours d'Elegance. In August 2021, the show presented a forum titled "Women Who Love Their Cars." Although female collectors and motorsports luminaries had frequently appeared at past shows, the stand-alone forum marked a first in the concourse's seventy-year history. "I can't think of a year when we haven't had women involved in showing cars—and I started here in the mid-1980s," says Mrs. Button. In 2021, for example, Anne Brockinton Lee, trustee of the highly regarded collection assembled with her late husband, was expected to field as many as a dozen cars at Pebble Beach.

The Pebble Beach Company Foundation offers Phil Hill and Jules "J." and Sally Heumann scholarships, named, respectively, for America's first Formula One champion and longtime Concours participant, and the Heumanns, he having served as co-chair of the event from 1972–1999. In 2021, the Foundation announced a new scholarship in automotive communications honoring well-known *Road & Track* photojournalist John Lamm. Not surprisingly, much of the foundation's assistance goes to young people pursuing careers in preservation and restoration, often at institutions such as McPherson College in Kansas or San Francisco's Academy of Art University. All of the above are open to women.

"It makes a lot of sense," Ms. Button says. "Basically, our show is an historical celebration, and many of the people engaged in restoring classic vehicles are at or near retirement age. We want the next generation, regardless of gender, to share in and contribute to what we love."

In 2021, Petersen Automotive Museum in Los Angeles launched an incubator program targeted at California-based, women-owned start-ups in the automotive industry. Limited to new firms with less than five employees, the initiative offers three-month mentorships and access to Petersen's extensive network of partners and sponsors. It hopes to foster entrepreneurial women engaged in a wide range of car-related fields, including engineering and product development, interior and exterior design, and even publishing and rideshare ventures. "This is a one-of-a-kind effort," says Diane Parker, vice president of Hagerty Drivers Foundation, which is advising the museum. "We want to empower and develop visionaries. This isn't about 'women in a man's world,'" insists Ms. Parker, who credits a pair of older "gearhead" brothers with nurturing her own automotive interests. "So what if it's a woman? It's about human beings living their passion!"

Maria Antonietta Avanzo, "Queen of Motors," could not have said it better.

5

RISING STARS AND HIDDEN GEMS

PART ONE:
AMERICAN CARS

"All American cars are basically Chevrolets."

Herb Caen, San Francisco newspaper columnist

"If you're in this game solely to make money, you're really a car dealer more than a car enthusiast," wrote Aaron Robinson when introducing Hagerty's first Bull Market List in 2018—the insurer's annual compilation of cars expected to outpace the market over the coming twelve months. "For the rest of us, we're all about listening to the heart, which usually talks a lot louder than the head. Certain cars just have that organ on speed-dial and there's not much we can do about it." For what it's worth, this *NextGen Guide* stands squarely on the side of the heart, especially those belonging to millennials, Gen Xers, and even Zers. Collectively, they represent the fastest growing cohort among car enthusiasts. And, for their shared passion, the future.

To remain sane and solvent, of course, our brains and pocketbooks must constrain our hearts. As a result, readers won't find many Ferraris, McLarens, Lamborghinis, or 8-liter Bentleys on the following pages. They won't see prewar Duesenbergs, Delages, or Delahayes, or postwar Packard Caribbeans either. Ditto for pickup trucks, station wagons, aluminum trailers, mahogany speedboats, and, with a few exceptions, cars with four doors. Any of those conveyances can be rare and collectible, but given our purposes we'll have to pass. You won't be seeing two-wheel vehicles either, so no motorbikes, scooters, or motorcycles. By and large, NextGen buyers aren't rich; they want classic cars they can love, live with, and occasionally even drive to the grocery store (while parking very carefully!), not just look at.

Thus, in compiling the following three chapters we've tried to cull some American, European, and Japanese cars we think represent good value and offer a potential return on investment, be it modest or massive. But first

and foremost, they are fun to drive! Though we've mixed in a few surprises, many of our choices are drawn from Hagerty's annual Bull Market List, plus some from our own experience as lifelong car guys. In the process, we've learned to respect internet sources. It's worth noting that when Hagerty introduced its first Bull Market List—based on 2017 data—Bring-a-Trailer.com was just emerging from adolescence. Today, the popular website is a billion-dollar-a-year, market-shaping goliath. Other helpful informational resources have included Edmunds, classic.com, Jalopnik.com, *Road & Track*, *Classic Motorsports*, *Grassroots Motorsports*, and *Car and Driver*, among others.

By all means, please consider our lists and suggestions as beginning points, not final destinations. And be sure to—as the Brits say—carry on from there. They should be considered appetizers, which we hope you will sample, tinker with, flatly reject, or pursue on your own. For example, one may quarrel with our inclusion of the once humble Porsche 912 but not the more powerful 911 in all its classic iterations. We believe the first-time NextGen buyer may find the four-cylinder model an easier starting point, driving wise and budget wise. We think the 912 fits our matrix—mostly cars that capture the heart but won't break the bank. And we hope you'll find cars that beg *you* to drive them. But always remember, as Hagerty's 2020 Bull Market List warned, the only thing crystal balls do reliably well is fail to predict the future.

Note regarding cars detailed on the following pages: Hagerty average values are stated as they appeared in December 2021. Additional information can be found at https://www.hagerty.com/valuationtools, where car values are ranked No. 1, Concours; No. 2, Excellent; No. 3, Good; and No. 4, Fair. The reader is urged to also consult other sources, such as https://bring-a-trailer.com and www.Classic.com, and *Sports Car Market* in the course of their research. Keep in mind an old car adage: Paying top dollar for a great automobile is the cheapest money a collector will ever spend. Example: The Hagerty average value for the 1993 Cadillac Allante featured in these pages barely touches $10,000. But a pristine, near-new barn find recently crossed the auction block for four times that much.

1993–2002 PONTIAC FIREBIRD FIREHAWK

A hopped-up, hyped-up descendant of the John DeLorean–parented, famously Burt Reynolds–driven Pontiac Firebird, the early '90s Firehawk was vigorously reimagined by GM's go-to mod-shop SLP (for Street Legal Performance) to include a 350-horsepower V-8, beefed up suspension, improved flow-through exhaust, and a more rounded, voluptuous body. The changes helped the car zip from 0 to 60 in a smidge over or under 5 seconds, depending on who was in the wheelhouse. According to NADA, Firehawks sold for around $26,700 in 2002, the last year they were new. Hagerty reported a "huge spike in interest in these cars" when it named the Firehawk to its newly created Bull Market List in 2018. Request for insurance quotes had doubled the year before, with most of that interest coming from Gen Xers and millennials. Values continued to climb in the following year. "It (the Firehawk) kind of came out of nowhere," the reviewer reported, pegging the car's then current value range from $24,100 to $31,300.

PONTIAC FIREHAWK

Engine:	V-8, 5,733 cc
Power:	335 hp @ 5,200 rpm
Torque:	350 lb-ft @ 4,000 rpm
Weight:	3,500 lb
Power-to-weight:	10.4 lb/hp
0–60:	5.1 sec
Top speed:	153 mph
Price when new:	$26,700
Hagerty average value:	$17,800

Be aware that automotive technical specifications may vary slightly according to their source and a given model's ultimate market destination.

Things may have cooled a bit since then, making the rare cars, if no longer Hidden Gems, possible Still-Rising Stars. In fact, a black-on-black '95 Firehawk with 40,000 miles went for $22,000 at Mecum Glendale in early 2021. Though below Hagerty's midpoint, that was nearly $6,000 more than a Bring-a-Trailer buyer paid in 2017, a figure most BaT commentators considered "well-bought" at the time. "Fun and reliable cars for not a ton of coin," said one kibitzer. Recalled another: "At my summer job in high school a guy that lived close by would drive by in a Firehawk . . . You know that feeling you get when you see a car that gives you the tingles? That Firehawk was mine. My dad would tell me, 'Son, if you want a car like that, you better get good grades and study hard in college.' So in a way, lusting after the Firehawk got me through college."

Only around 4,000 Pontiac Firehawk coupes and convertibles were built by GM-SLP during the car's seven-year run, making them, as one car guy pointed out, rarer than some Ferraris. Nearly half came with six-speed manual gearboxes. And they were faster than flies at a picnic. Critics dinged the cars for their cheapo plastic interiors and hard-to-find Firehawk-original parts, but most conceded they were relatively straight ahead mechanically and could be, as one put it, "as fun as the old muscle cars but with modern amenities."

1966–1970 OLDSMOBILE TORONADO FIRST GENERATION

America's first front-drive passenger car since the ill-fated Ruxton and Cord models of the 1930s, the Toronado was named *MotorTrend*'s Car of the Year in 1966. "Never in the fourteen-year history of this award has the choice been so obvious and unanimous," the magazine's

editors wrote. "The Toronado is symbolic of a resurgence of imaginative engineering and tasteful styling in the U.S. auto industry." Given its handling advantages in inclement weather, *Car and Driver* enthused, "the Toronado inspires more driver confidence than any American luxury car we can think of."

The Toronado was also General Motors' first unitized body, which made it roughly twice as stiff as an Olds 98, said *Car and Driver*, permitting occupant-enhancing reductions in road noise and engine vibrations. Although the car's fastback design restricted rear headroom, the interior's all-flat floor allowed seating for six in surprising comfort for a coupe. Most importantly, however, the first-generation Toronado was arguably GM's best-looking two-door. Besides its peekaboo headlights, recessed bumpers, and sculpted nose, the Toronado boasted a svelte, pillarless profile, which managed to make the 2.5-ton vehicle appear simultaneously slinky and a bit sinister. To top it off, the stylish wheels offered an unmistakable homage to the 1936 Cord 810.

"As the owner of a '66 Toronado, let me say these are a joy to drive and people go bananas over it whenever it leaves the garage or when parked at a car show," wrote BaT commentator Toro66 during bidding for a modified Toronado in 2019. The car, a heavily customized "Fitch Phantom," went for $19,500 in 2019.

Although a customized first-gen Toronado convertible featured in the *Mannix* television series sold for $101,000 in 2019, Hagerty reports an average value of $17,700 for No. 3 (Good) condition cars. Condition No. 1 1966 Toronados—that is, "best in the world" specimens—are rated at $42,100. In fact, a No. 1 1967 model with fewer than 20,000 verified miles went for $60,500 at RM Sotheby's Palm Beach auction in 2020. Actual prices in 2021 ranged from $12,500 to $23,100.

Readers should note that we are limiting our recommendation to *first-generation* Toronados.

Later chunky-bumpered, naked-headlight models lost the visual and visceral appeal of what GM heralded as America's first personal luxury car. There were reasons Oldsmobile sold more than 40,000 Toronados in 1966, and high among them were the car's refinement and cornering ability, quite amazing for a large car of its era. Later models also suffered from safety issues—think funky airbags and flaky shoulder belts mixed with sudden acceleration. As with other Hidden Gems, buyers should search for lower mileage cars and keep watch for rust in the trunk and elsewhere caused by clogged drain lines.

1966–1970 FIRST-GEN TORONADO

Engine:	V-8, 6,964 cc
Power:	385 hp @ 4,800 rpm
Torque:	475 lb-ft @ 3,200 rpm
Weight:	4,500 lb
Power-to-weight:	11.7 lb/hp
0–60:	8.6 sec
Top speed:	130 mph (approx.)
Price when new:	$4,997 (1966)
Hagerty average value:	$17,700

1996 CHEVROLET CORVETTE GRAND SPORT

A salute to the fearsome Corvette Grand Sports that thrived in early 1960s SCCA racing, the first production Corvettes to bear the GS designation were instant classics three decades later. Only 1,000 individually numbered Grand Sports were produced, 810 coupes and 190 convertibles. As did their racing forebearers, the '96 models came in a single color combo: a dazzling Admiral Blue divided by a fat white stripe down the middle. Double red hash marks slashed the driver's side above the front wheel well and wider tires clearly separated the GS from vin ordinaire Vettes.

Although *Road & Track* complained about the '96 Grand Sport's "truckish" handling at low speeds, "the Vette seems to thrive on velocity," the magazine conceded, "feeling lighter, more secure, and more composed as the scenery starts to blur. With improved fiberglass-to-steel bonding techniques and strategically placed reinforcements . . . the Corvette's structure now takes full advantage of its delicate-looking forged aluminum suspension pieces and ultrawide tires."

A ragtop Grand Sport showing 111 miles brought $73,700 at Mecum Indianapolis in May 2021, but our vote for a better bargain came two months earlier on Bring-a-Trailer. That's when a one-owner coupe with 9,000 miles and a six-speed stick went for $35,000. "Fabulous car and way fast and underrated," said one BaT commentator. Another called

1996 CORVETTE GRAND SPORT

Engine:	V-8, 5,733 cc
Power:	330 hp @ 5,800 rpm
Torque:	340 lb-ft @ 4,500 rpm
Weight:	3,400 lb
Power-to-weight:	10.3 lb/hp
0–60:	5.2 sec
Top speed:	168 mph
Price when new:	$37,225
Hagerty average value:	$24,200

a fourth-generation Corvette with a manual transmission "a rare find for sure." To top it off, the car was one of only 190 coupes with a black leather interior and additionally boasted a Bose sound system, four-wheel disc brakes, and ebony 17-inch wheels.

Hagerty ballparked the car's value at $36,100 to $49,500 when posting the GS

on its Bull Market List in 2019. "Just 1,000 examples built in one year means these cars are rare, fast, and distinctive," said its valuation team. "In a Corvette—in fact, in most cars—those factors add value. Plus, most Grand Sports were treated as collector cars from new, which means lots of low-mileage choices out there." NextGen searchers would do well to hunt for one of the 217 coupes delivered with red seats.

1996–2002 DODGE VIPER GTS

"Generation Xers and millennials are now 64 percent of the quotes on this car," reported Hagerty's Valuation Team in naming the Viper to its Bull Market List for 2020. That assessment was borne out during the first six months of 2021 by the fact that only two Vipers failed to make their auction reserves. Indeed, eighteen Vipers sold during that period and for the most part their prices climbed at a 45-degree angle, reaching a combined total of $1.8 million. At midyear, a 1998 model, purchased new by

Aerosmith drummer Joey Kramer, offered in original condition and showing just 18,000 miles, sold for $46,000 on Bring-a-Trailer. Newer models continue slithering upward, Hagerty noted, with record sale after record sale. A 2017 Viper GTS-R Final Edition ACR sold on BaT for $407,000 in the summer of 2021. Car number 001 of 100 built to celebrate the snake's 25th anniversary, the vehicle showed just 57 miles on the odometer and its window sticker read $145,340.

To be clear about one thing: the Viper is not meant for the faint of heart. "The Viper has a reputation for being crude and uncompromising," Hagerty conceded, "but it's a driver's car and a visceral experience." In its 1997 review, *Car and Driver* asked, "What's the fastest street car made in North America? The new Corvette is quick," the magazine replied in answering its own question, "but Dodge's swaggering, 488-cubic-inch V-10 Viper is quicker still. 'After you,' is not something this brawler says to anybody . . . Its acceleration flattens eyeballs." Later in its road test, *Car and Driver* noted that the Viper needed little more

1997 DODGE VIPER GTS

Engine:	V-10, 7,990 cc
Transmission:	6-speed manual
Power:	450 hp @ 5,200 rpm
Torque:	490 lb-ft @ 3,700 rpm
Weight:	3,400 lb
Power-to-weight:	7.6 lb/hp
0–60:	4.2 sec
Brakes F/R:	Disc/disc
Price when new:	$66,000
Hagerty average value:	$56,000

than 30 seconds to travel from 0 to 170 miles per hour.

As Hagerty observed, the original Viper represented a collaboration by some legendary names from autodom: Chrysler president Bob Lutz, chairman Lee Iacocca, and "performance consultant" Carroll Shelby. Lamborghini helped in developing the car's aluminum block engine. The GTS's styling echoed Shelby American's Daytona Cobra coupes of 1965. Thirty-three years later, Viper GTS coupes scored a 1-2 class finish at Le Mans, ensuring their own vaunted heritage. Unlike those earlier brutish beasts, however, the Viper came with power windows and air-conditioning. A real roof, airbags, and a refined interior were offered beginning in 1998; fixes to leaking piston rings and other improvements made the cars attractive to more buyers. "The outlandish design has aged well, and attrition has worked in the Viper's favor, meaning there aren't a lot of good ones left," Hagerty said. "The early cars are now seen as desirable."

Fewer than 7,000 Vipers were produced, making them fairly rare. "They are fast, easy to live with, their looks still stop folks in their tracks . . . a supercar with pickup-truck durability and great club support," summed up Hagerty. First-time purchasers should be sure to have good, reasonably new rubber on any car they buy; those fat tires need to be grippy, especially for first-time drivers.

2001 FORD MUSTANG SVT COBRA

You gotta say, "Wow, 'All these snakes!'" when you see the ready-to-strike coiled cobra atop this baby's engine block. Rated a "buy" by Hagerty in 2019, Ford's upgraded, New Edge design 1999 SVT Cobra Mustang was fully sorted by 2001. Boasting a full 320 horsepower from its hand-assembled, aluminum block V-8, this was the first-generation Mustang with fully independent rear suspension. Coupled with the already stiffened SN-95 Fox platform, the result was a ride that, according to *Car and Driver*, "endears itself to road racers by keeping the back end well-planted." Moreover, as *Road & Track* enthused, the engine is robust enough to pull the car "like a freight train all the way up to its 6,800-mile redline."

These cars may not boast the full-out racing goodies of the ultra-low-production R-designated Mustangs, but they don't cross the block at $100,000-plus either. Typical 2021 sales for SVTs included a highly original 1998 model showing 33,000 miles, auctioned by Mecum, and a smashing 2003 dealer-sold specimen in triple-black with high-end alloy wheels. These cars went for $33,000 and $32,700, respectively. A 1995 SVT Cobra showing less than 400 miles with 17-inch wheels, disc brakes, and a five-speed transmission brought $32,250 on Bring-a-Trailer. The virtually newborn car included its original window sticker and dealer-installed plastic floor coverings.

As Hagerty noted, these cars carry the prestige of Ford's high-performance Special Vehicle Team, and earlier models are "still a

2001 FORD MUSTANG SVT COBRA

Engine:	V-8, 4,601 cc
Transmission:	5-speed manual
Power:	320 hp @ 6,000 rpm
Torque:	317 lb-ft @ 4,750 rpm
Weight:	3,285 lb
Brakes F/R:	Disc/disc
Price when new:	$28,190
Hagerty average value:	$10,600

bargain for now . . . the difficulty is finding one that wasn't driven hard and put away wet."

1971–1980 INTERNATIONAL HARVESTER SCOUT II

"Classic SUVs are soaring," Hagerty declared in assembling its 2020 list of ten collector cars whose values were on the rise. "Younger buyers don't just want cool, they want usable cool. And classic SUVs, especially later ones, fit the bill." Accordingly, fully a third of the four-wheel vehicles included on the firm's Bull Market List for that year were sport utility vehicles.

The venerable International Harvester Scout is highlighted partly for its nostalgic American rural-life heritage, but mostly for its impressive features, performance, and value. As Hagerty noted, with a tighter turning radius than a contemporary Jeep Cherokee and a foot shorter than a Ford Bronco, the Scout II is "compact and nimble, capable of thrashing a tight trail or nuzzling into any mall parking spot without worry."

Founded in 1907 as a builder of agricultural vehicles and equipment, International Harvester began producing its people-carrying Travelall, basically an all-metal, two-door station wagon, in the early 1950s. The Scout 80, essentially a four-cylinder pickup with a fold-down windshield, came along in 1960, and the Scout II was introduced in 1971. The II's redesign gave the buyer the choice of a soft-top, hardtop, removable steel top, or straight pickup. By 1976, front-wheel disc brakes were standard

along with power steering, (available) third-row seating, and four engine choices, including a V-8 boasting 168 horsepower.

"For those seeking something different," said a DriveLine.com reviewer, "the Scout II is especially appealing. With so many different configurations . . . and with stock parts still available through major retailers like NAPA, ownership of this IH SUV is less expensive than one would expect. As a trail rig, too, their strong fundamentals and simplistic mechanicals make them good candidates for off-roading, even in a modern context. When everyone else is driving a Jeep—and with Bronco prices through the roof—why not consider the other classic SUV?"

Though lagging Ford Bronco and the Chevy Blazer, Scout values seem to be on a steady climb. Hammer prices ranged between $30,500 and $64,000 on Bring-a-Trailer in 2021. Earlier IIs were particularly successful, with a '79 going for $82,500 at Mecum Indianapolis and a handsome model in gunmetal gray (but with unknown mileage) sold for $55,000 on BaT. However, especially

1979 INTERNATIONAL HARVESTER SCOUT II

Engine:	V-8, 5,654 cc
Transmission:	3-speed automatic
Power:	168 hp @ 3,800 rpm
Torque:	288 lb-ft @ 2,000 rpm
Weight:	3,800 lb
Power-to-weight:	22.6 lb/hp
Brakes F/R:	Disc/drum
Price when new:	$7212
Hagerty average value:	$32,900

with early cars, buyers should carefully assess candidate purchases for rust. "Most Scouts rotted away," said Hagerty, "but you're starting to see them being restored." Gen Xers accounted for 56 percent of the firm's quote requests for Scouts in 2019, "and if Gen X likes them, values are going to go up."

1993 CADILLAC ALLANTE

Perhaps no car on this list will generate more controversy than the Italian-bodied Allante, a car Cadillac hoped—in vain, as it turned out—would compete with Mercedes's venerable 107 series SLs. The bad news is that for five of its six-year run, the naysayers were justified. The good news is that in its final iteration—which wound up accounting for some 25 percent of the Allante's total output—it became, if not a great car, a potentially good one. Today, if carefully chosen and maintained, a well-sorted '93 Allante can qualify as a true Hidden Gem—beautiful, collectible, reasonably cheap to buy, and fun.

"Everyone likes the styling and looks of the '93 Cadillac Allante," one owner wrote on Classic.com, "yet the handling is phenomenal. This car turns on a dime and positively hugs the road while doing so. It has lightning-quick acceleration and stops relatively quickly. I always thought the Camaro Z28 was the best-handling car I had ever driven. That was until I sat in the cockpit of the '93 Cadillac Allante. It's in a class by itself."

So what made the difference? To begin with, Cadillac's all-new, all-aluminum 295-horsepower Northstar V-8. With its dual-overhead cams, the front-drive engine easily revved to its redline at 6000 rpm. If not neck-snapping fast, the Allante could hit 60 miles an hour in a jot over six seconds—still frisky performance for the early 1990s. In addition, a properly maintained '93 Allante could deliver impressive durability; contemporary owners attest to logging 200,000 to 300,000 miles on their Northstar Allantes. However, eagle-eyed upkeep is a must; Northstar mechanicals—especially head gaskets—need consistent oversight. Other positive revisions for '93: upgraded front and rear suspension and power steering; road-smoothing, magnetically managed shock absorbers; traction control; and improved antilock disc brakes. Offered only as a soft-top—a 60-pound aluminum hardtop could be had as an (expensive) option—the '93 was the first and only Allante with single-pane side windows.

1993 CADILLAC ALLANTE

Engine:	DOHC V-8, 4,599 cc
Transmission:	4-speed automatic
Power:	295 hp @ 5,600 rpm
Torque:	290 lb-ft @ 4,400 rpm
0–60:	6.1 seconds
Top speed:	140 mph
Weight:	3,720 lb
Brakes F/R:	Disc/disc
Price when new:	$59,975 (not including top)
Average Hagerty Value:	$9,900

All in all, the changes were impressive enough to result in the '93 Allante—stock except for mandated safety gear—being chosen official pace car at that year's Indy 500. From the beginning, it had been a dubiously costly venture, with 60 Pininfarina bodies at a time loaded onto Boeing 747 jets and flown from Italy to the United States for assembly. When the end came, however, many Allante employees and devotees were saddened to learn a "business decision" had been made to drop the car just when, on so many levels, it was coming into its own.

Recent '93 Allante prices have varied widely, from the mid-teens to $30,000 to $40,000 for low-mileage, highly original cars. An apparently never sold polo green model, with 126 verified miles, was found stored in a failed California dealer's warehouse. Locked inside were its intact handbook, window sticker, and other manufacturer's "addenda." The car, including the expensive aluminum hardtop, was auctioned for $40,700 by Barrett-Jackson in Las Vegas on June 18, 2021.

2009 PONTIAC G8 GXP

"If you want an affordable, full-size, rear-wheel-drive sedan with American muscle and European élan, the 2009 Pontiac G8 GXP is the only game in town," Edmunds declared in reviewing what would become the 102-year-old marque's swan song.

And what an out chorus it was.

For starters, the GXP featured a 402-horsepower Corvette-based 6.2-liter V-8 and an available six-speed manual transmission. Couple that responsive power with MacPherson struts in front and multilink suspension in back and the buyer got a ride that rivaled high-end European sports sedans. "More than just raw power," a Pontiac press release exulted, "the GXP delivers the sophisticated yet exciting driving experience that enthusiasts expect in a car costing far more than the GXP." Translation: At a tad under $40,000, the GXP, whose Pontiac styling cues were more than faintly reminiscent of BMW's big 7-series sedans, was a bargain.

Moreover, as Edmunds noted, the closer you looked, the better it got. Inside, in place of often plasticky Pontiac interiors, the GXP featured a full panel of round-faced, color-coordinated instruments; bolstered two-tone bucket seats; a leather-wrapped sports steering wheel and gearshift lever; and, as if to rub salt in already open wounds at Stuttgart and Dingolfing, a high-end, 230-watt Blaupunkt audio system.

Although Hagerty pegged GXP values between $40,700 and 47,800 and rising in 2019, recent sales appear to have drifted lower. A Panther Black model with a stick shift, 96,000 miles, and a damaged front spoiler managed to hit $27,500. However, in early 2021, two other models stalled out in the mid-twenties without making their reserves, despite showing significantly lower mileage and, in one case at least, being ultra clean.

2009 PONTIAC G8 GXP

Engine:	V-8, 6,162 cc
Power:	415 hp @ 5,900 rpm
Torque:	415 lb-ft @ 4,600 rpm
Weight:	4,000 lb
Power-to-weight:	9.6 lb/hp
0–60:	4.7 sec
Top speed:	146 mph
Price when new:	$39,900
Hagerty average value:	$28,600

As Hagerty noted, Pontiac's swan song model is likely the closest thing we'll ever see to a four-door Corvette and among the most powerful factory Pontiacs ever made. Moreover, with only 1,829 GXPs produced, most people don't even know it existed. If that doesn't qualify it as a Hidden Gem, we don't know what would.

1970–1973 CHEVROLET CAMARO Z28

"Underappreciated 1970–1973 Chevy Camaro Z28s are a decent value," wrote Hagerty's Andrew Newton in October 2018. We think the same could be said today but with a bit more enthusiasm. In fact, as *Hemmings Motor News*'s Richard Lentinello gushed about the GM-birthed early '70s pony car, it had "one of the most inspiring exterior designs that has ever been applied to a mass-produced automobile."

Simply put, the early '70s Z28 was drop-dead gorgeous. European touches—a flowing, long-nosed body; cellular, Ferrari-inspired grill; and split-eyebrow bumpers that could have graced an Alfa Romeo Giulietta—made the car seem lighter and smaller than it really was. And even though the Corvette-based LT1 V-8 had been reduced from 360 to 245 horsepower by the end of its run, these second-generation Camaros remained formidable on the street.

Here's what twenty-one-year-old "Zer" Gabriel Markarian, a software engineer, told *Hemmings* about his decision to buy a bright yellow Z28: "I test-drove plenty of similarly priced modern cars before deciding to buy a classic—the new MX-5 Miata, V-6 or Turbo-4 Mustang, and Scion FR-S—all of which are capable cars in their own right, with looks to match. But that actually ended up becoming the problem . . . anything new and sporty is so capable these days, you have to be going so fast [to enjoy the car] that the authorities will take notice. The thing about owning a '73 Camaro is that it's special even when you start it up. At 20 miles per hour going straight, you have more sensation than at 60 mph going around a rotary [roundabout] in a new Miata. You are present when you drive these cars; there is nothing opaque about being in one."

Nearly half of the nearly 28,000 Z28s were built in 1973. Today, even fully or partly restored cars seem to hover in the $20,000 to $40,000 range. Still, a 40-miles-post-restoration model, in Smoke Mesquite Brown (a Toyota color) with custom leather interior, 18-inch polished

1973 CHEVY CAMARO Z28

Engine:	V-8, 5,733 cc
Power:	245 hp @ 5,200 rpm
Torque:	280 lb-ft @ 5,200 rpm
Weight:	3,300 lb
Power-to-weight:	9.6 lb/hp
0–60:	7.4 sec
Top speed:	125 mph
Price when new:	$3,713
Hagerty average value:	$29,500

wheels, and a four-speed stick, made $69K at a late 2020 *Hemmings* online auction. Truly original cars are getting scarce, and those split-eyebrow bumpers carry as much as a 20 percent premium, according to Hagerty.

6

RISING STARS AND HIDDEN GEMS

PART TWO:
EUROPEAN CARS

"Money may not buy happiness, but I would rather cry in a Jaguar than on a bus."

Françoise Sagan, French playwright, novelist, and screenwriter

Since 2015, Bring-a-Trailer.com, the popular online website devoted to buying and selling classic cars, has compiled an annual list of the ten automobiles that achieved the highest prices during each preceding year. Given BaT's global reach, it seems worth noting that, of the sixty vehicles listed from 2015 to 2021, all but eight were manufactured in one of just three countries: Germany, Italy, or England. Put another way, European cars won fully $20 million of the $24.4 million taken in by the website's top ten earners. For the record, Porsche dominated the marques, with twenty of the highest earners, followed by eight Ferraris, five Mercedes, and four each for Jaguar and Lancia. Recording onesies and twosies were BMW, Maserati, Aston Martin, Austin-Healey, Lamborghini, Rolls-Royce, and Bentley.

Thus emerges a question, stark and sizzling, against our sunny sky of choices: What makes European cars so desirable? How can we account for their dominance in the minds of collectors and enthusiasts? Are the reasons real and tangible, nurtured by fundamental differences in quality of manufacture, style, and performance? Or are they merely based on fuzzy perceptions, nurtured by media, snobbery, outright prejudice, and even utter myth?

In a 2019 promotional essay, the owners of Kirberg Motors, a half-century-old German auto-repair specialist in San Francisco, listed six reasons why European cars are superior to, well, every other car on the planet. The Kirberg list: 1) better fuel efficiency, 2) more advanced technology, 3) higher resale value, 4) superior engineering, 5) greater longevity, and 6) greater aesthetic appeal.

It's hard to agree with *all* of these contentions. For one thing, European automakers tend to export mostly their premium cars, which could impact several of the factors cited above. Moreover, one must remember that European automobiles are typically more costly to maintain than American or, even more certainly, Japanese machines. Still, anyone who has examined, for example, a Mercedes R107-series SL sports car would be hard put to dispute its superior build quality. For eighteen years, the Stuttgart cars did not undergo a single significant body panel change. Porsche, Jaguar, Alfa Romeo, and others have historically enjoyed similarly long-lived runs for their designs. Moreover, each marque was visually distinctive. A Jaguar never looked like an Aston, nor a Lamborghini like a Ferrari. Contrast that with American cars' collective stampede for fins, "continental kits," and horsepower in the 1950s and '60s.

We think the best course is to respect European cars for what, at their best, they are: well-built vehicles that are nice to look at and fun to drive. As in the previous chapter, by drawing on Hagerty's Bull Market Lists, other selected sources, and our own experience, we will strive to help NextGen readers make quality choices, uncover a few bargains and beauties, and, perhaps, reveal a possibility or two not previously imagined.

2000–2006 AUDI TT QUATTRO

The first-generation Audi TT belongs on every NextGen buyer's short list of desirable Euro classics. The Quattro's leather-loaded interior oozes quality, from its (optional) baseball-stitched bucket seats to its aluminum-accented instrument panel—including speedo, odo, tacho, ammeter, oil, fuel, and temperature gauges—to its (after 2001) six-speed stick that slides into your palm like a small avocado. On

the outside, the Audi's rounded body may give off distant whiffs of Beetle, but there's really nothing that looks like it. As Hagerty declared in naming the car to its 2021 Bull Market List, the TT's design "sent every other automaker scurrying for tracing paper." And all signs show that would-be purchasers, boomers especially, are catching on. The number of online visitors checking out the insurer's TT values jumped by 175 percent during the last six months of 2020.

Buyers could choose between two turbocharged, transverse-mounted, four-cylinder, 20-valve engines, rated at 180 and 225 horsepower, respectively. After 2003, a 3.2-liter V-6 was offered. Sharing the same platform as the Volkswagen Golf, all TTs came with four-wheel power disc brakes and fully independent suspension. All-wheel drive was optional on the 180-horsepower cars and standard on the 225-horsepower and V-6 cars.

"Thanks to its rigid body, compliant suspension, and all-wheel drive, the TT Quattro has always been a capable handling machine," *Road & Track* wrote in a 2004 review of the V-6, "but with the extra oomph, the car's driving dynamics come to life. Once you're off the line, the TT 3.2 Quattro accelerates smoothly and briskly to its 6600-rpm redline, accompanied

2000–2006 AUDI TT QUATTRO COUPE

Engine:	3.2-liter V-6
Transmission:	5-speed manual
Power:	250 hp @ 6,300 rpm
Torque:	236 lb-ft @ 6,300 rpm
Weight:	2,900 lb
Power-to-weight:	16.1 lb/hp
Price when new:	$30,500
Hagerty average value:	$9,800

by a pleasant throaty exhaust note. Audi claims that it will run to 62 mph (100 km/h) in 6.4 seconds." *R&T* continued to extol the car's "first-rate" cornering and the "formidable low- and mid-range punch of the engine." With the enhanced traction provided by AWD, it added, "the TT spits out of corners quickly" with minimal body roll.

Early (1998 and '99) TTs were recalled after a series of accidents caused by erratic handling at high speed. Resulting factory modifications included the addition of electronic stability and anti slip regulators, a rear spoiler, and suspension system modifications. The Audi TT was nominated for the North American Car of the Year Award in 2000 and was included in *Car and Driver*'s Ten Best list for 2000 and 2001. From 2019 to 2020, Hagerty reported a 58 percent increase among fifty-seven- to seventy-five-year-old buyers—possibly signaling growing interest among better-heeled collectors—who were often willing to bid up for low miles. "The big sales needed to solidify the TT as a collector car could come soon," the insurer warned in 2021. As that was written, a spate of high-mileage 2000 to 2006 TTs were still going for around $10,000 at various auctions. But a super clean 2001 ragtop with a six-speed stick and showing just 13,000 original miles brought $32,000 on Bring-a-Trailer. "You won't see mine for sale as long as I am alive," declared BaT commenter and TT owner 1-Scrambler. "I am sixty-seven years old and have owned many nice and now collectable cars. The TT is my favorite."

1967–1969, 1976 PORSCHE 912

Always a stand-in, never a star, the four-cylinder 912 was introduced in 1967 to replace the venerable 356, which had been discontinued two years earlier. In 1970, the 912 was itself replaced by the 914 as Porsche's entry-level offering. When the 914 was phased out in 1976, the 912 E (for "Einspritzung," fuel injection) returned for a one-year encore. All told, some 32,000 912s were produced.

Despite its entry-level status, and its existence in the shadow of what some consider the greatest sports car of all time, the 912 has grown to enjoy a kind of cult status over the

1976 PORSCHE 912

Engine:	1.6-liter flat four
Transmission:	4-speed (optional 5-speed) manual
Power:	90 hp @ 4,900 rpm
Torque:	173 lb-ft @ 4,700 rpm
Weight:	2,127 lb
Price when new:	$4,700
Hagerty average value:	$37,000

years. Though sporting some 40 horsepower less that the 911, the 912 was also 200 pounds lighter. With nearly all that weight reduction occurring behind the rear axle, the 912 was far less subject to sudden oversteer and tail-happy handling than its sibling. "Under certain conditions," wrote Andrew T. Maness on Jalopnik.com, "the four-cylinder car could actually be driven faster than its more expensive, more powerful stablemate."

But there was, and is, more to little sister than cranking through curves. As Mr. Maness waxed, "There's nothing in the 912 that doesn't need to be there, and that's one of the most attractive parts of the whole package. It's minimalist without being devoid of comfort, and relaxed without being boring . . . houndstooth seats, a single driver's side mirror, a large thin-rimmed steering wheel—this car is a time machine." The 912 E was even moderately fast, achieving 60 miles per hour in 9.7 seconds and boasting a top speed of 112 miles per hour. As Hagerty noted, Porsche 912s seem to enter and leave the market in spurts, resulting in erratic patterns in their pricing. Though uncertain mileage cars with paint chips and color changes hover in the $40,000 to $50,000 range at online auctions, low-mileage cars can top $70,000 and concours-quality

examples $100,000-plus. A 1969 soft-window Targa showing 5,000 miles with a five-speed transmission and a known two-owner history sold for $110,000 on Bring-a-Trailer in 2021. Coupes generally achieve at least 20 percent less than Targas. By 1969, 912s had enjoyed a series of minor safety and weight distribution tweaks; the wheelbase had been lengthened by 2¼ inches to improve handling.

"That these cars remained overlooked for so long because they had a four-cylinder engine is a testament to how ridiculous the enthusiast community can be," wrote Mr. Maness after testing a 912. "Driving the 912 is undeniably special."

1948–1954, JAGUAR XK 120 SE

Though its prices have waned in recent years, this automotive icon was named to the Hagerty Bull Market List for 2021. A key reason: Gen X valuation inquiries, a leading indicator of buyer interest, had risen by a third since 2019. After mid-decade sales that hit and in some instances exceeded $200,000, in recent years most 120s have settled into the $100,000-plus range—putting them in Rising Star territory.

That still might seem like a steep climb for NextGen pocketbooks, but consider the 120's storied place in automotive lore. Introduced at the 1948 London Motor Show, the handbuilt aluminum roadster was intended to show off the new 3.4-liter engine inline six planned for installation in the firm's sedans. However, the sports car's stunning beauty and performance were not to be denied. Eventually, more than 12,000 steel-bodied 120s were produced in roadster, coupe, and "drop head" (convertible) versions.

At its debut, the new Jaguar was the fastest production car in the world. Its six-cylinder, dual-overhead cam engine generated some 160 horsepower and could power the car to speeds

of 120-plus miles per hour—hence its "120" designation. In 1951, a factory-sponsored, aluminum-bodied car, designated the XK120C (for "competition") gave England its first Le Mans victory in twenty years. The Jag finished 77 miles ahead of its nearest competitor, and set lap and 24-hour records of 105 and 93 miles per hour, respectively.

Remo Biaggi, a veteran vintage car owner and racer, recounts tooling along Northern California's rugged coast in a friend's 120: "I expected the car to feel like so many '50s automobiles I've driven, somewhat truck-like. While I was a bit nervous initially, that quickly drained away. Confidence grew as the car carved up Highway One, surprising me with its responsiveness. There was none of the lag or ponderousness I'd expected. It was so remarkably balanced with abundant torque that I quickly caught up to any vehicle ahead.

1954 JAGUAR XK 120 SE

Engine:	3.4-liter I-6
Transmission:	4-speed manual
Power:	180 hp @ 5,000 rpm
Torque:	203 lb-ft @ 2,500 rpm
Weight:	2,900 lb
Power-to-weight:	16.1 lb/hp
Price when new:	$3,945
Hagerty average value:	$101,000

When we turned off onto Mountain Home Road—to the really challenging twisties—I felt anticipation and a readiness. What transpired up and down that mountain will last me the rest of my days. I pushed, it gave back. I could go into tight, off-camber corners with increasing confidence, just nicking apexes. Even had a few 'moments,' when the rear got a bit loose on gravel, but she could be collected up with steering inputs and throttle. Great torquey acceleration out of those corners. The gearbox was a newer five-speed and with double clutching was a delight, smooth and precise, incredible fun. I felt this is what a great sports car is all about: involvement."

According to Hagerty, the Jag is "one of the loveliest British cars ever made; sturdy bits; nobody will ever ask you why you own it." However, the reviewer continued, it has "challenging ergonomics for taller people. [It was] too cheap for too long, so many were abused—due diligence and a Jag Heritage Certificate are key." A few years ago, this seminal sports car fell from grace in the market—but that drop only served to bring out the enthusiasts who recognize the Jag as a great deal, especially in No. 3 condition. In the past year, interest from Gen X has picked up.

1980–1981 TRIUMPH TR8

They, we'll never know who, called it the "Junior Jaguar." Somebody else, who we'll also never know, called it the "English Corvette." Nobody, on the other hand, ever called it pretty. But that was then—when the Triumph TR8 was new. Now, more than four decades later, the winds may be shifting. Triumph's last sports car arguably may have been its best, Hagerty's Jonathan Klinger told Bloomberg News in 2019. A skeptic might have argued that coming after the firm's universally loathed TR7, there was nowhere to go but up. But even when the TR8 debuted, there was a lot of good press. *Road Test* magazine named it the Best New Sports Car of 1980, saying its new Rover-sourced, Buick-derived, aluminum V-8 "transforms the car." *Car and Driver* gave the

TR8 a cover, claiming it represented "nothing less than the reinvention of the sports car." And *Road & Track* praised its torquey power plant as 80 percent punchier than a TR7, 25 percent stronger than a Datsun 280Z, and 22 percent better than a Porsche 924 Turbo. The new Triumph, said *R&T*, "will outrun most every other sports sedan and sports car this side of $15,000."

Road & Track and *Car and Driver* clocked

0 to 60 performance at a tad over 8 seconds. TR8 upgrades included power steering, meatier brakes, improved weight distribution, and a standard five-speed manual transmission. Nonetheless, sales were disappointing and British Leyland halted production in 1981, marking the end of nearly six decades of Triumph motor cars. With less than 3,000 cars produced, the TR8 was the rarest of them all.

To Mr. Klinger and others, the above factors arguably help make the TR8 the best Triumph investment. Moreover, NextGen purchasers—like collectible car buyers before them—are seeking cars that evoke memories from their youth, cars from the '70s, '80s, and '90s. As a result, vehicles from those decades have seen marked increases in auction values, largely driven by younger buyers.

Although some contemporary critics carped about its wedge shape and cheapo interior, even

1980–1981 TRIUMPH TR8

Engine:	3.5-liter V-8
Transmission:	5-speed manual, optional automatic
Power:	133 hp @ 4,900 rpm
Torque:	168 lb-ft @ 4,700 rpm
Top speed:	135 mph
Weight:	2,654 lb
Price when new:	$11,000
Hagerty average value:	$11,300

with these alleged flaws time has been kind to the TR8. Think how cool those '70s plaid seats would look at a RADwood event. Moreover, although it lacked Triumph's traditional polished wood dash, the TR8 is roomier and more practical. It's also considerably faster than its predecessors—TR8s were winning SCCA races long after their manufacturer's demise. Finally, TR8s are rare, surprisingly modern, and surprisingly cheap, especially compared to Britain's other V-8 roadster, the Sunbeam Tiger. Hagerty No. 2 Excellent TR8 convertible values hover around $20,000.

1968–1973 OPEL GT

"Our car may not win at Le Mans or Sebring, but it's great if you just want to have some fun," read a then-contemporary magazine ad for the German car that looked for all the world like a scaled-down Corvette Stingray. As your friendly Buick salesman quickly confessed, however, any resemblance ended there. With a standard

67 horsepower motor it took 16.7 seconds for the sleek little coupe to reach 62 miles per hour. (A later 90-horsepower motor helped cut that to just over 10 seconds.)

Still, the cute little Opel *was* fun. It came with somewhat vexing Solex carbs that could be switched to preferable Webers; a four-speed stick shift for which the factory offered an optional five-speed ZF; power-assisted front disc brakes; and a front-mid engine/rear-wheel-drive design that improved weight distribution and made for crisp handling. Behind its wood-simulated steering wheel, the dashboard boasted rocker switches and a full panel of instruments. Among the car's most endearing features were its hidden headlights, which opened and closed manually.

"Once ensconced inside a GT," wrote one reviewer, "you find the car to be surprisingly roomy, unless you're extremely tall or portly. The two-seat cabin can't be called airy, but neither is it claustrophobic. The Opel is not a particularly fast piece, but because it's so low to the ground, you get a zoomy feeling quite literally in the seat of your pants. With rear-wheel drive and a solid axle, it's a car that you can toss around, always reasonably certain of a recovery if the back end should break away."

GT prices have been hovering in the mid-teens of late, but a pristine, fully restored '73 with an automatic transmission and showing less than 15,000 miles hit a hammer price of $30,240 at RM Sotheby's in 2020. Hagerty advised that, when shopping, "harden your heart against the rusty ones with missing headlights." The good news: worldwide, 101,000 GTs were produced and most parts are available via OpelGTsource.com.

Summed up *MotorTrend*: With a promotional push from Bob Lutz, design input from Corvette's legendary Clare MacKichan, mechanicals from Germany, and a French body, "the Opel GT is a piece of affordable international automotive history. And those

1968–1973 OPEL GT

Engine:	1.1, 1.9-liter I-4
Transmission:	4-speed manual, 3-speed automatic
Power (1.1l):	67 hp @ 6,000 rpm
Power (1.9l):	102 hp @ 5,300 rpm
Torque (1.1l):	58 lb-ft @ 4,000 rpm
Torque (1.9l):	115 lb-ft @ 3,100 rpm
Weight:	2,000 lb
0–60:	10.1 sec (1.9l)
Top speed:	110 mph
Price when new:	$3,395
Hagerty average value:	$9,200

froggy pop-up headlights make for even more fun after dark."

2000–2004 PORSCHE BOXSTER S

According to an Edmunds Expert Review, the Boxster S has "a mid-engine design and classic Porsche styling, not to mention sublime steering and brakes," giving the Boxster "a unique combination of traits that few cars can match at this price point." The verdict from *Car and Driver*: "So much fun, it's got to be a sin." In the late 1990s, Porsche hired a team of former Toyota consultants to launch an entry-level model reminiscent of the 1970s' 914. The result was a $40,000 (base price) sports car with, pronounced Hagerty, "low, curvaceous lines, a wailing flat-six, and highly organic handling." For another ten grand, the buyer got an "S," which meant a bigger engine—250 versus 217 horsepower—a glass-windowed convertible top, crimson calipers on Carrera-sourced brakes, a proper glovebox, aluminum

interior accents, leather-wrapped shifter and brake levers, and door pulls. Developed in tandem with the new 911 of that era, the Boxsters—the first ground-up new Porsches in two decades—helped make their company the world's most-profitable-per-unit producer of automobiles.

Boxsters have gone for as little as the low five figures in recent online sales, but expect to pay more for cars in good condition. A primo S brought $31,500 on Bring-a-Trailer in July 2021. The flawless 2003 Seal Grey Metallic model showed just 18,000 miles and boasted a six-speed manual along with a power-operated, glass-windowed top. One BaT commenter noted that Porsche had recently announced its

2000–2004 PORSCHE BOXSTER S

Engine:	flat six, 3,179 cc
Power:	250 hp @ 6,200 rpm
Torque:	229 lb-ft @ 4,500 rpm
Weight:	3,000 lb
Power-to-weight:	11.6 lb/hp
0–60:	5.3 sec
Top speed:	162 mph
Price when new:	$50,695
Hagerty average value:	$14,300

1998–2002 BMW M ROADSTER

An Edmunds.com reviewer called it "the world's fastest tennis shoe. It steers like a go-kart and has one of the sweetest motors available." Frank Markus, writing for *Car and Driver* in August 2001, said the little BMW "comes closest to capturing the bugs-in-the-grin roadster ambience of yore. One sits tall in the saddle, with less car up around the shoulders . . . Our editors who own a Jag E-type and a Sunbeam Alpine roadster felt right at home."

If the M nailed it in retro looks and feel, however, there was nothing vintage about its performance. Introduced with a somewhat anemic four-cylinder engine, BMW quickly stepped up the power plant to inline six cylinders, initially offering 240 and then 315 horsepower. With an 11.5 compression ratio and just 3,141 pounds to lug, the car achieved 0 to 60 in around 5.3 seconds. Motorbiscuit.com's Jimmy Brown called that sans turbo or supercharger performance "prodigious."

Moreover, as Mr. Brown noted, the roadster's appeal didn't stop there. The cockpit's low belt line made it easy to hang an elbow out a side window, and the M's no-frills interior was easy to admire. Plain, round-faced gauges told the driver all they needed to know, the car came standard with a five-speed manual transmission, and there were no superfluous buttons, navigation screens, or CD players. The only concessions to modern comfort were heated bucket seats, a premium sound system, and a power convertible top. Revised underpinnings improved suspension response, said *MotorWeek*. "Convertible chassis flex was minimal . . . the lightweight M roadster rocketed out of corners and down straights." Oversize four-wheel discs brought the speedy little car to a halt precisely 162 feet after hitting 72 miles per hour.

Perhaps the most compelling argument for the M roadster is its current status as a stone

unveiling of a twenty-five-year anniversary S replica—at a price of $118,000!

Said Hagerty: "Why this car got cheap: It has the early ugly headlights, the intermediate shaft bearing problem, and a reputation for poor build quality. But fifteen years after production ended, there's a fix for the bearing, and most survivors will have had it done. Many people who could buy a $50,000 car new are the kind who do the maintenance and keep records . . . You can be lapping up the top-down delights of a Boxster while enjoying nearly perfect ergonomics and carving your favorite road to ribbons—all for $15,000 or less. The Boxster is everything a Porsche should be: luxurious, thrilling, and, above all, fun."

killer bargain. The same car with a steel top—only 678 larger engine coupes were imported into the United States—costs nearly twice as much and doesn't come with fresh air. A Classic.com survey of 164 publicly reported roadster sales from 2016 to 2021 showed average prices hovering just above $20,000—$20,526 to be precise—with a low sale of $6,929 and a high of $40,500, the latter being a peerless 2002 example in Black Sapphire Metallic with 29,000 miles. Contrast those numbers with the coupe, whose 145 sales over the same period generated an average price of $39,380 and respective lows and highs of $12,100 and $100,678—just about double.

Said Hagerty: "The styling, which seemed overwrought all those years ago, has aged surprisingly well. The divinely fluid clutch-pedal movement; the pure, linear throttle response; and the familiar 'valvey' hum of the BMW inline-six are all reminders of that period in the 1990s and early 2000s when seemingly everything BMW M touched was pure gold." The coupe had already popped, and roadster values were up 22 percent by decade's end on the later 315-horsepower cars and 31 percent (starting from a lower value) on the earlier 240-horsepower cars. Yet good M roadsters are still half the price of good M coupes.

1998–2002 BMW M ROADSTER

Engine:	I-6, 3,246 cc
Transmission:	5-speed manual
Power:	240 hp, 315 hp @ 6,000 rpm
Torque:	236 lb-ft @ 3,800 rpm
Weight:	3,100 lb
Power-to-weight:	12.9 lb/hp
Brakes F/R:	Disc/disc
Price when new:	$42,770
Hagerty average value:	$23,500

1999–2005 FERRARI 360 SPIDER

"Someday we'll look back and say, 'I can't believe how cheap these were,'" reflected one Bring-a-Trailer commenter in early 2021 after a black-and-tan 2001 Ferrari 360 S with 6,000 miles and a six-speed transmission crossed BaT's block for $118,000.

In fact, Classic.com reports prices for manual tranny 360 Spiders averaged $103,543 from 2017 to 2021. That was $20,000-plus higher than for paddle shifters, a difference perhaps also accounted for by the fact that only about a fourth of the 2,389 U.S.-market Spiders came with manuals. In fact, not a single manual 360 has sold for under $100K since early 2020. Aside from a still-standing five-year high of $154,000, achieved by Gooding & Company in 2017, the recent top price for a stick-equipped 360 Spider was $138,360, recorded on BaT in May 2021.

Considering a 360 Spider's $170,000 list price when new, that still seems like "buy" territory for NextGeners with sufficient funds. Especially since, when it debuted, the 360 was a seminal product in more ways than one. In fact, as the first Ferrari built using a high-strength aluminum space frame, it was the car that ushered Maranello into the modern era. Ironically, the 360 was also the last Ferrari to employ the Dino 308 GT4-based V-8 and, according to Autotrader. com, the final model to offer a stick shift as standard equipment.

With its long wheelbase, mid-mounted engine, fully independent suspension, and wide-track front end, the Spider offered refined handling. Meanwhile, as Hagerty noted, located behind the cockpit, the "hedonistically transparent" engine cover "left no doubt as to

2002 FERRARI 360 SPIDER

Engine:	V-8, 3,586 cc
Transmission:	6-speed, dual-clutch
Power:	400 hp @ 5,500 rpm
Torque:	275 lb-ft @ 4,500 rpm
Weight:	3,100 lb
Power-to-weight:	7.8 lb/hp
Brakes F/R:	Disc/disc
Price when new:	$170,779
Hagerty average value:	$106,000

the star of this show. Underneath red intake plenums that looked like a pair of nice gams in red spandex," the 40-valve 3.6-liter engine could propel the Italian screamer from 0 to 60 in 4.4 seconds.

NextGen buyers will want to make certain the 360's infamous cam variator issue has been resolved. Ferrari offered a simple fix but not all models received the update. Also be sure to check dates on the most recent change out of engine belts—service can cost five grand and should be done every three to five years. The good news is that, unlike earlier Ferraris, the engine itself won't need to be pulled.

1972–1974 ALFA ROMEO GTV 2000

The storied name of Alfa Romeo was still in ascendancy as the 1960s drew to a close. The firm's all-aluminum GTA coupes had won successive European Touring Car Championships under the direction of ex-Ferrari engineer Carlo Chiti, who led Alfa's Autodelta racing arm. The 1960s-developed Tipo 33 TT 12 racer, with its flat-12 engine, would go on to win the World Sportscar Championship. And the butterfly-doored Alfa Romeo Tipo 33 Stradale,

when introduced in 1967, was the world's fastest production car.

So it was that, as Alfa Romeo released the final evolution of its Giulia coupes in 1972, its mainstream production cars reflected that rich legacy. The Gran Turismo Veloce 2000 featured a peppy, all-aluminum, double-overhead cam engine; a smooth-shifting, alloy-encased five-speed transmission; and sure-stopping, power disc brakes at all wheels. Everything considered, the GTV ranked among the world's most advanced four-cylinder drivetrains. Moreover, the car's crisp, Guigiaro-penned curves and creases and ample greenhouse offered classically simple lines and airy visibility. Its interior, with polished wooden steering wheel, tuck-and-roll bucket seats, and pop-out back windows, conveyed a sense of casual luxury.

But what's a GTV 2000 like close up, half a century later?

First, the good news: a well-sorted 2000 GTV can be easy to live with. Its tight steering, tough underpinnings, and strong brakes deliver an impressive ride and confident handling. Like

1972–1974 ALFA ROMEO GTV 2000

Engine:	I-4, 1,962 cc
Transmission:	5-speed, limited-slip differential
Power:	130 hp @ 5,500 rpm
Torque:	134 lb-ft @ 3,000 rpm
Weight:	2,264 lb
Power-to-weight:	7.8 lb/hp
0–60:	8.9 sec
Top speed:	122 mph
Brakes F/R:	Disc/disc
Price when new:	$6,700
Hagerty average value:	$41,300

all Alfas of that era, its camshafts are driven by durable stainless steel chains, and its sodium-filled valves rarely need resurfacing. Finally, vitals like spark plugs and oil filters can be changed by just about any home mechanic who can lean over an engine bay.

Sadly, there's bad news as well. Far too many GTVs have been abused, raced to exhaustion, poorly repaired, left outside to rust, or incorrectly restored. One "restored" 1973 model, for example, recently garnered more than $75,000 on Bring-a-Trailer, despite displaying incorrect taillights, wrong-year "flying buttress" seats, and other non-original lapses. Other misbegotten "mods": "naked" bumpers, and GTA-style wheels, door handles, and four-leaf quadrifoglia decals.

Some advice: look for a bumpered car (they're there for a reason and, unlike a Sprint Speciale or 1900 coupe, a GTV looks naked without them) and one that's been maintained by a long-term owner who kept their beloved chariot garaged and in at- or near-original condition. Resto-mods are bringing strong money these days, but the long-term market for tricked-up, non-original cars is difficult to predict. Alfa built almost 40,000 GTV 2000s, so gems are out there, you'll just have to kiss some frogs to find one. And never buy a GTV you haven't personally seen and driven.

Supporting our advice were a pair of five-year high GTV hammer prices, as reported by Classic.com, one for a 1969 1750 model showing $170,000 in receipts that RM Sotheby's auctioned for $117,600 in 2019, the other a '72 GTV 2000 that sold for $108,650 on the UK's Collectingcars.com in December 2020. Both vehicles represented 100 percent correct, as-new-when-original restorations. More typical, however, was the $42,000 BaT sale of a modded-out, bumperless '74 GTV in April 2021.

7

RISING STARS AND HIDDEN GEMS

PART THREE: JAPANESE CARS

"I remember testing those early Lexus sedans and coupes for the first time. I knew instantly that something seismic had happened in the automotive universe."

Jack Keebler, auto journalist and former quality team leader for GM

If early 1990s Lexus sedans and coupes were seismically prophetic, they'd been preceded by an even earlier quake: the 1967 Toyota 2000GT. Jointly developed and built with Yamaha, the 2000GT was like no other Japanese car before it. Designed by Albrecht von Goertz, of BMW 507 fame, the six-cylinder 2.0-liter GT featured dual-overhead cams, seven main-bearings, triple side-draft carbs, and a five-speed manual transmission. Four-wheel disc brakes and rack-and-pinion steering completed the picture. Capable of speeds of more than 130 miles per hour, Toyota's first GT also became Japan's first supercar.

Millions of moviegoers saw a chop-top version of the 2000GT in the 1967 James Bond film *You Only Live Once*—actor Sean Connery was too tall to fit in the coupe. But millions more never saw the car at all; by 1970 Toyota had dropped the car as an expensive sidetrack. In all, only 337 models had been built (almost all right-handers), and only 60 of them made it to American shores. When introduced, the GT listed for $7,230, more than a Porsche 911 or a Jag E-type. Today, 2000GT prices are celestial, averaging in the mid-600Ks and topping out at around $900K. As Randy Nonnenberg, founder and president of Bring-a-Trailer, told the *New York Times* in 2019, "Japanese cars are getting to be full-fledged collectibles,"

In reviewing those first generation Lexus six- and eight-cylinder coupes, for example,

Hagerty's Ronan Glon lauded the cars as having been built in an era when "luxury meant a quiet, comfortable cabin, not a television-sized screen propped up on the dashboard . . . in 2020, cars pegged in the SC's segment are often so laden with features as to be daunting to drive."

Many of the cars in this chapter are included in what Hagerty defines as "up-and-coming" Japanese collectibles. Millennials are driving this market, Brian Rabold, the firm's vice president of Automotive Intelligence, observes. "If a young person is only going to have one fun car," he told the *Times*, "these models are familiar, usable, and affordable. They check all the boxes."

Japanese cars boast another highly desirable trait: uncommon reliability. Even high-mileage, decades-old models can supply today's enthusiast with years of dependable fun. One well-kept 1991 Nissan 300 ZX, for example, recently displayed an online asking price of $23,000, despite having logged 187,000 miles during its two-decade history.

1993–1998 TOYOTA MK IV SUPRA TURBO

Nine years after the last 2000GT had come and gone, the Toyota Supra arrived as a Celica sibling only to be quickly dismissed by *Car and Driver* as a "make-believe Monte Carlo." By the 1993 arrival of its fourth generation, however, as one Edmunds reviewer declared, the Supra was "a serious driving machine."

Sharing the Lexus SC300's legendary 2JZ-GTE twin-cam inline six, the Supra used double turbos to add 100 horses and cut its 0–60 times to as low as 4.6 seconds. As MotorTrend.com's Alex Leanse observed in 2019, "The Supra Turbo was one of the best sports cars of the '90s . . . quarter miles passed as quickly as 13.4 seconds at trap speeds of up to 107.1 mph. For comparison, a Corvette ZR-1 dispatched the quarter mile in 13.6 seconds at 106.0 mph. Only a Ferrari 512TR's lateral acceleration of 1.01 g was higher than the Supra's sticky 0.98 g."

1993–1998 TOYOTA MK IV SUPRA TURBO

Engine:	I-6, 2,997 cc, turbocharged
Power:	320 hp @ 5,600 rpm
Torque:	315 lb-ft @ 4,000 rpm
Weight:	3,400 lb
Power-to-weight:	10.6 lb/hp
0–60:	4.6 sec
Top speed:	160 mph
Price when new:	$42,800 (1994 Turbo)
Hagerty average value:	$62,200

Not everybody cheered the new Supra's looks, however. Edmunds found "the hyena-like front styling" disconcerting. "The Supra has a wild-eyed look, and the huge air intake below the bumper needs only a row of white teeth to guarantee that small children would never pass within twenty feet of the front end." Mixing his or her wildlife metaphors, the same reviewer wrote, "The image is one of a shark ready to strike, and you find yourself wishing you had a spear to jab into one of the headlights."

Toyota Supra Turbo prices averaged $71,860 over 123 public sales during 2017 to 2021, reports Classic.com. The lowest recorded sale was for $21,575 on Bring-a-Trailer in 2018. The highest, an off-the-charts outlier at $550,000, came via Barrett-Jackson in 2021 for a '94 Supra Turbo used in the movie *Fast & Furious*.

Said Hagerty: "This is the poster car for the *Fast & Furious* (see above) and Gran Turismo generation. It may even pass the Acura NSX, because unmodified examples are so rare." Pros include Toyota reliability and all-day driving comfort. However, too many modded-up cars have "been hacked and chewed by shadetree tuners."

2004–2009 HONDA S2000

The enduring popularity of Honda's S2000 was demonstrated in 2020 by the number of times its manufacturer emphatically denied rampant rumors that the car *U.S. News & World Report* twice named the Best Affordable Sportscar would be revived on the tenth anniversary of its demise. To the disappointment of S2000 enthusiasts everywhere, no such commemorative edition was in the works or being planned.

In its own look back in 2021, *MotorTrend* asked of the S2000, "Is it the legend we remember it to be?"

"In 2003," answered *MotorTrend*'s Nick Yekikian, "we said Honda's goal was to develop a convertible two-seater with quick acceleration, taut handling, crisp shifting, great braking ability, and looks to kill. We feel it's reached the goal. We loved every minute we spent with the S2000 all those years ago, and if you handed us the keys to one today there's little chance anything would be different."

By the introduction of its second generation in 2004, the S2000 offered a double-overhead cam inline four cylinder engine with variable valve timing that delivered 237 horsepower and redlined at 8,900 rpm. Oh, and did we mention a six-speed manual transmission was standard equipment?

Further modifications brought the horsepower up and dropped the revs down, giving the car greater torque and cutting 0–60 times from 5.6 to 4.9 seconds. The S2000's top speed was nearly 150 miles per hour. Handling was also improved, thanks to reduced oversteer, a stiffened subframe, independent front and rear suspension, stability control, and four-wheel anti lock disc brakes. By the time production ceased, more than 100,000 S2000s had been produced.

Hagerty values current No. 1 (Concours) 2004–2009 S2000 cars at $43,000;

2004–2009 HONDA S2000

Engine:	I-6, 2,997 cc, turbocharged
Power:	320 hp @ 5,600 rpm
Torque:	315 lb-ft @ 4,000 rpm
Weight:	3,400 lb
Power-to-weight:	10.6 lb/hp
0–60:	4.6 sec
Top speed:	160 mph
Price when new:	$42,800 (1994 Turbo)
Hagerty average value:	$62,200

No. 2 (Excellent) and No. 3 (Good) machines at $32,000 and $18,500, respectively. Recent sales bear those figures out. A spotless 11,000-mile 2007 model in Laguna Blue Pearl sold for $44,750 on Bring-a-Trailer in July 2021. A month earlier, a "highly original" S2000 from the same year, with ten-spoke alloy wheels and red-and-black leather interior with matching carpeting and trim, pulled in $44,250.

Said one BaT commentator of the blue S2000: "For those that think this car, in a super desirable color and practically brand new, was expensive, come see me in another couple years!" Hagerty called the S2000 "a direct competitor of the Porsche Boxster, Mercedes-Benz SLK, and BMW Z Roadster. All of those cars cost much more than the Honda, and none of them has garnered the same kind of enthusiastic following." Indeed, since early 2020, the insurer has tracked a sharp increase in S2000 values, especially for No. 1 and No. 2 condition cars. The much rarer (fewer than 700 were built), stripped-for-competition S2000 CR—for "Club Racing"—goes for much more; a 2009 model with 985 miles sold for $112,000-plus on BaT in 2021.

1990–2005 ACURA NSX

"Along with my S2000s and my NSX, I also have a 911 Turbo with 11,000 miles," wrote one Bring-a-Trailer commenter during a summer 2021 auction that saw a 2005 Acura NSX sell for $131,000. "While the 911 is an amazing car, I still prefer the NSX."

Car and Driver called it "a fighter jet for the road." But we think someday someone will name the mid-engined head-turner the best collectible supercar to take to the grocery store.

"This sophisticated, well-built, high-performer provides plenty of thrills, yet is a fairly practical day-to-day car," wrote Consumerguide.com in a 2020 retrospective. "Given Honda's minimalist philosophy, its engineers . . . targeted . . . curb weight. The NSX lays claim to being the world's first mass-produced car to feature an all-aluminum body. As a result, it enjoyed one of the best power-to-weight ratios among its primary competitors, despite being powered by a relatively small V-6 engine (3.0 liters at first, with an upgrade to 3.2 liters in 1997).

The NSX was also an early beneficiary of Honda's innovative Variable Valve Timing &

1990–2005 (FIRST-GENERATION) ACURA NSX

Engine:	VTEC V-6, 3,179 cc
Power:	290 hp @ 7,100 rpm
Torque:	224 lb-ft @ 5,500 rpm
Weight:	3,069 lb
0–60:	5.2 sec
Top speed:	170 mph
Price when new:	$84,000
Hagerty average value:	$82,800

Lift Electronic Control System (VTEC) engine. Launched in 1989's Acura Integra, the VTEC design aimed at achieving higher performance at high rpms and better fuel economy at low rpms. VTEC brought the NSX whisper-close to meeting its goal of delivering 100 horsepower per liter and—remarkable for a supercar—doing so while sipping fuel at an average of 25 miles per gallon.

Most commenters felt the winner of a July 2021 Bring-a-Trailer auction got a bargain when he paid $50,000 for a '94 NSX. The clean, twenty-three-year-owner car showed 96,000 miles and had a factory four-speed automatic transmission, rather than the standard five-speed (a six-speed came along a year later), which may have been a drag on value. Basing their estimates on a 2001 3.2-liter NSX, Hagerty pegged No. 1 Concourse values at $145,000, with No. 2 Excellent, and No. 3 Good values falling to $131,000 and $63,900, respectively. Classic.com reported twenty-nine NSX sales over the 2016 to 2021 period ranging from a low of $59,000 to a high of $162,400.

"VTEC Hondas have long been known to take all kinds of abuse and just keep on running," Hagerty said in an overview, "and when it does come time for service, the NSX is not as much of a drain on the bank account as some of its European rivals, making it a highly appealing way to get into exotic car ownership, just like when it was new." Then there's that wide-as-the-world view from the driver's seat, like sitting in the cockpit of a fighter jet, as one reviewer said. Even so, it's still an old car and it's still a lot of money. As always, a wise buyer will consider a clear-eyed look at a prepurchase mechanical inspection required reading.

1970–1974 DATSUN 240Z, 260Z

Perhaps no single automobile can lay stronger claim to its rightful place in the pantheon of Japanese classics than Datsun's first-generation "Z" cars, known in Japan as the "Fairlady." More than 220,000 240 and 260 Zs were produced (168,000 and 53,451, respectively). Both cars were fitted with single overhead cam, inline six-cylinder engines with side-draft carburetors, and respective horsepower ratings of 150 and 154 at 6000 rpm. The 240 had a top speed of 130 miles per hour; the longer, heavier 260 of 125. Zero to 60 times were also similar at 8.7 and 8.5 seconds, respectively.

As Japan's first for-real, big-volume sports car, the 240Z had it all, wrote *MotorTrend*'s Julia LaPalme in 2020: "Performance, Japanese reliability, an affordable sticker." As a less costly echo of the Jag E-type, it also boasted such attributes as "a long hood and a short deck, a revvy overhead cam six, independent suspension, rack-and-pinion steering, a four-speed transmission, and full round gauges—real sports car credentials."

Added Topgear.com in a 2019 team review that called the 240Z "a reliable, plentiful, and easy-to-drive classic": "You're more likely to use it than leave it cowering in a garage . . . And every time . . . you'll get the full satisfaction out of it because this sweetly balanced little coupe

loves to be opened up. It's just as appealing now as when it conquered the world fifty years ago."

In January 2020, a spectacularly original 1970 240Z, in racing green with a brown vinyl interior and 21,750 miles, sold on Bring-a-Trailer for $310,000, as recorded by Classic.com, proving what can happen when two bidders desperately want the same vehicle. However, *average* 240 auction prices have hewed to a more reasonable $29,149 through 295 sales over the past five years. The 260s averaged $20,997 with a top sale of $57,357 over the same 2017–2021 period, the website said.

The 240Z forever changed the "cheap junk" regard in which most Americans held Japanese cars, said Hagerty. Its smooth engine and independent suspension made the Z "go and handle as well as it looked." Hagerty estimated Concours (i.e., Best-in-World) 240 values at $92,400 while pegging Excellent and Good values at $63,200 and $23,600, respectively.

1970–1974 DATSUN 240Z, 260Z (DATA SHOWN FOR '74 260Z)

Engine:	SOHC I-6, 2.4 liter, 2,565 cc
Power:	162 hp @ 6,000 rpm
Torque:	148 lb-ft @ 4,400 rpm
Weight:	2,300 lb (240Z); 2,425 lb (260Z)
0–60:	7.8 sec
Top speed:	127 mph
Price when new:	$5,479
Hagerty average value:	$16,100

The 260s are cheaper. Although parts are widely available for both models, Z cars without rust are increasingly difficult to find. Shop carefully.

1993–1997 TOYOTA LAND CRUISER FJ80

Plucked from Hagerty's Bull Market List for 2021, this rugged beastie makes the "Rising Star" category for good reason: insurance quotes requested for FJ80s went up 162 percent from 2018 to 2020, with millennials and Gen Xers accounting for most of them. In 2021, the Land Cruiser's final year, it seemed an especially appropriate time for a bow to the 80 series, the last FJ with Toyota's indomitable, indestructible inline six and a hill-and-bump leveling solid front axle.

Besides being a four-wheel-drive vehicle, the 80 featured a central-locking differential that—in addition to front- and rear-locking diffs—gave it superior off-road capability. The new 24-valve, 4.5-liter engine produced 212 horsepower and 275 pound-feet of torque, making it a towing powerhouse. Coil springs in front helped smooth the ride.

Outside, the 80 lost some of its roughrider edges—a smoother, more modern exterior gave the Cruiser a fresher look. The interior included leather-trimmed seats, a rounded dash, primo audio gear, and air-conditioning. Post-1996, airbags and ABS brakes made for greater safety.

Especially in the face of huge FJ40-62 demand and prices, Hagerty suggested giving the 80 "a long, hard look . . . These machines are so stout, it's not uncommon to see one still going strong with 300,000 miles on the odometer—a result of Toyota building them to a standard, not a price" (somewhere, W. Edwards Deming must be smiling).

1993–1997 TOYOTA LAND CRUISER FJ80

Engine:	DOHC I-6, 4,477 cc
Power:	212 hp @ 4,600 rpm
Torque:	275 lb-ft @ 3,200 rpm
Weight:	4,760 lb
0–60:	12 sec
Top speed:	106 mph
Price when new:	$36,258 to $40,238
Hagerty average value:	$19,500

Hagerty Valuation Tools rate the FJ80 at $64,300 in Concours condition, $34,600 in No. 2 Excellent fettle, and $17,300 in No. 3 Good shape. In the course of seventy-one sales over the past five years, the venerable Land Cruiser averaged $26,449 with a low of $6,600, reported Classic.com. However, in June 2020, a 1994 model in Dark Emerald Pearl with precisely 1,000 factory-fresh miles went under Bring-a-Trailer's hammer for $136,000. Separately, one enthusiastic Edmunds reviewer reported putting 335,000 trouble-free miles on his 80. "Best car I ever had," he wrote. "The problem with this SUV is that it is so good you don't want to let it go. It drives better than many new SUVs coming right off the showroom."

1997–2001 ACURA INTEGRA TYPE R

Frequently cited as the best handling front-wheel-drive car of all time, the two-door Integra R's mostly plain vanilla looks belie its muscle and performance. As Hagerty noted, its 1.8-liter four-cylinder motor redlines at 8400 rpm, giving it the highest piston speed of any car in the world at the time and more horsepower per liter than a Ferrari F355. Honda's already potent VTEC design was bolstered by racy stuff like reshaped intake valves, molybdenum-coated aluminum pistons, and high-lift cams. The result? A normally aspirated output of 195 horsepower and 130 pound-feet of torque.

But more than just a screaming jungle beast, the Integra R's smooth five-speed manual gearbox, larger sway bars, revised springs and dampers, and stiffened chassis gave it handling so neutral it didn't feel like a front-drive car. "To say the Type R handles better than other front-drivers is to miss the point," wrote Hagerty, "which is to say that it handles better than just about anything."

Increasingly sought by millennials, Type R hammer prices averaged $29,864 in sixty-two sales over the past five years, reported Classic.com. At the top end, a Bring-a-Trailer sale brought $82,000 for a bone stock, one-owner, '97 model in Championship White with 6,000 miles. Hagerty reported that after a big post-2018 jump, average No. 1 (Concours) Integra R values have leveled off at $69,000, with No. 2 (Excellent) cars bringing $44,500 and No. 3 (Good) cars $29,000. As with many high-performance, relatively easy-entry cars, the trick is to find unmodified examples.

On the way to RADwood LA in 2019, *MotorTrend*'s Billy Rehbock recalled watching the tachometer climb toward redline as he drove on the Pacific Coast Highway near Santa Monica. "As the cam profiles changed, the engine note shifted from pleasant growl to an

2000 ACURA INTEGRA TYPE R

Engine:	I-4, 1,797 cc
Transmission:	5-speed manual
Power:	195 hp @ 8,000 rpm
Torque:	130 lb-ft @ 7,500 rpm
Weight:	2,600 lb
Power-to-weight:	13.3 lb/hp
Brakes F/R:	Disc/disc
Price when new:	$24,830
Hagerty average value:	$33,400

outright wail that could rip open the sky. It was so awesome that I actually let out a primal scream of my own."

1967–1972 MAZDA COSMO SPORT

For those who simply must have something rare in a Japanese car, few machines can equal Mazda's Cosmo Sport, made from 1967 to 1972. Just over 1,500 cars were built and none were officially sold in the United States— they were "JDM" cars, that is, for "Japanese

Domestic Market." Nonetheless, the Cosmo marked a true automotive milestone—the first successful production application of the rotary engine designed by German engineer Felix Wankel. Fifty years later, nearly two million vehicles had been produced with the unique spinning motor.

"Even though I spent a mere hour behind the wheel," wrote *MotorTrend*'s Tom Salt in a 2010 Cosmo retrospective, "I could tell everything about this car screams passion. Its luscious bodywork, eye-opening interior, rewarding steering, great ride quality, responsive engine

(when revved) . . . tugged at my heartstrings and got inside my soul. I couldn't just get out and walk away. I needed to distance myself from the Cosmo in stages, periodically looking back to take in the incredible curves and lines and reminisce about one of the most rewarding driving experiences I'll ever have."

Similarly, *Road & Track* called it "one of the coolest sports cars ever made."

It took years to get there. The initial Wankel motors shipped from Germany to Japan in 1962 quickly failed. Only after years of trial and error testing did Mazda engineers trace the

1967–1972 MAZDA COSMO SPORT

Engine:	982 cc, two-rotor Wankel
Transmission:	5-speed manual
Power:	130 hp @ 7,000 rpm
Torque:	103 lb-ft @ 7,500 rpm
Weight:	2,072 lb
0–60:	8 sec
Top speed:	120+ mph
Price when new:	$13,128
Hagerty average value:	$92,200

problem to faulty seals. According to company legend, one day an engineer stared at the pointy end of his pencil and came up with the idea of carbon-based seals, which ended the motor's persistent fuel leaks and unacceptable emissions. Further bench testing confirmed the superiority of a dual-rotor design in delivering stable torque.

As JDM cars, all Cosmo Sports are right-hand drive. Introduced in 1968, Series II cars featured a 982-cc, 128-horsepower, two-rotor engine with a single Zenith carburetor and a five-speed manual transmission. Suspension was improved and the car got a longer, smoother riding wheelbase. Capable of speeds over 120 miles per hour, Series II models accounted for just over half of total Cosmo production.

Cosmo Sports infrequently come up for sale, and when they do are expensive. A 1970 model with rare factory air-conditioning brought $73,700 in a no-reserve auction at Mecum Glendale in 2021. Two years earlier, however, a 1967 model went for a record $264,000. Hagerty valued No. 1 (Concours) condition Cosmos at $164,000, with No. 2 cars pegged at $132,00 and No. 3 vehicles at $92,200.

1989–1997 MAZDA MX-5 "NA" MIATA

"We never thought we were building a collectible car," Tom Matano, executive director of the School of Industrial Design at San Francisco's Academy of Art University, told the *New York Times* in 2019. As leader of the MX-5 Miata's original design team, he recalled, "We were inspired by small English roadsters like MGs, Triumphs, and Healeys."

For those who have actually driven a first-generation "NA" Miata, however, a better comparison might have been a 750 Series Alfa Romeo Giulietta Spider from the late 1950s—the Japanese car was that good. Both vehicles weighed a feathery 2,000 pounds give or take; had double-overhead cam engines and slick-shifting manual transmissions (the Mazda's a five-speed, the Alfa's a four); and a nearly perfect 50-50 weight distribution, which contributed mightily to their legendary handling.

Like the Alfa, the Miata steadily improved over the years, gaining a 1.8-liter engine in 1994, and another power boost in 1996. Top speed climbed to 118 miles per hour and 0–60 times fell below 9 seconds. Limited "M" and "R" edition cars variously offered more horsepower, stiffer springs, and anti roll bars, along with front and rear spoilers. All told, Mazda built and sold more than 220,000 first-generation Miatas, ranking it among the most popular sports cars in history (add in all the post-97 Miatas and it *is* the most popular sports car in history) and theoretically building a huge candidate pool for collectors at still-reasonable prices.

Except it's not that easy. As Kurt Ernst, himself an "NA" Miata owner, pointed out in *Hemmings*, "Time and depreciation have not been kind to the model, and in their most affordable days, many were altered by tuners in the name of more speed, improved handling, or simply the 'right stance.'" Cheap Miatas

were frequently turned into racing cars, and the model is so popular for this purpose that the Sports Car Club of America (SCCA) even has a dedicated Spec Miata class. Miatas driven year-round (or not properly maintained by owners) were particularly susceptible to the tin worm, with rusted fenders and rocker panels common flaws.

The best news: Finding a good one will be worth the effort. Here are some descriptors used by *MotorTrend*'s Amberly Jane Campbell after spending 650 miles behind the wheel of a one-owner, 1990 Miata in stellar condition: "delightfully predictable roadholding; cheap to buy, cheap to run, cheap to repair; doesn't leak; hasn't ever been a manual top easier to put up or take down; everything works and if it doesn't is easy to set right."

Hagerty put current first-generation Miata MX-5 No. 1 (Concours) values at $30,600, with No. 2 Excellent cars at $18,200 and No. 3 Good Miatas at $9,200. "M" and "R" edition cars go for 20 percent higher. In June 2021, a very clean, no-accidents, "highly original" MX-5 Miata showing 23,000 miles sold for $11,750 on Bring-a-Trailer.

1989–1997 MAZDA "NA" MIATA

Engine:	DOHC, 1,839 cc
Transmission:	5-speed manual
Power:	128 hp @ 7,000 rpm
Torque:	110 lb-ft @ 7,500 rpm
Weight:	2,182 lb
0–60:	8.7 sec
Top speed:	118 mph
Price when new:	$14,000
Hagerty average value:	$10,100

As *Hemmings* summed up, in the thirty years since its introduction, "praise for the world's most popular sports car hasn't really dimmed. The first-generation models, dubbed 'NA' in Miata-speak, were built from 1989 to 1997, and some would argue that they're the purest distillation of the reimagined roadster. From a price and availability perspective, there's no better time than now to add one to your garage or driveway."

8

BUYING YOUR FIRST COLLECTIBLE CAR *SUCCESSFULLY*

"I spent my first paycheck on a vintage Mercedes."

Jennifer Aniston

MBZ 280 SL: Jen's first paycheck

For two years the cream-colored 280 SL had been wearing a "For Sale" sign near Fred Segal's shop (the late fashionista-founder of the "L.A. Cool" jeans-and-blouses look) on Melrose Avenue in Los Angeles. And every time the young actress passed the old automobile, she admired it.

"I remember thinking, 'Wouldn't it be great if I could buy that car one day," Jennifer Aniston recalled during a 2021 interview with *InStyle*'s Christopher Luu. "And then the first year of *Friends* happened, and I was like, 'You know what, I'm going to buy that antique car, 'cause I've always loved that car.' It might have been like $13,000."

That decision, however, only marked the beginning of Ms. Aniston's soon-to-be short journey. Instead of purring contentedly all the way home, her big "I've made it" impulse purchase soon uttered a statement of its own: an ugly money-sucking sound. "I don't even actually think I made it home," the actress recounted. "So it might've honestly just been a shell of a car, and I was the sucker to finally buy it. The amount of work I had to put into that car just to make it drive a block was . . ."

You can probably fill in the rest of the story. Ms. Aniston's painful experience explains why, in this chapter's title, we added the word *successfully* in italics. That same title also explains why our initial admonition to a first-time classic car buyer is to proceed—another italicized word—*carefully*. Buying old cars is not for the faint hearted and ill prepared.

So just what *are* the first steps in the successful purchase of a classic car?

1. Begin by asking yourself some basic questions. How do you plan to use the vehicle? Will your new classic be your only driver? If so, the best course may be to stick to post-1990s cars, with special consideration given to Japanese models. If, on the other hand, it's planned as strictly a Sunday driver, the candidate field widens considerably. And if it's intended as a restoration/show car project, that can open a wider range still—not to mention a can of money-eating worms—because no matter the age or condition, you're planning to set aside the funds and time to bring your beauty to its full promise—right? And this assumes you've got a reliable clunker to get you to work and back, pick up pizza, and haul the kids to school, the park, and dance lessons.

2. Once you've determined the year, model, and marque you'll pursue, steep yourself in information about that specific vehicle. How much do you know about the car? It sounds as if Ms. Aniston didn't know much more about her Mercedes than its model number and color. If you're lusting for an early Mustang, be aware that its front suspension is Falcon/Comet based and may need replacement. Thoroughly research the object of your desire. That doesn't mean perusing the pages of *Consumer Reports*—there's little chance you'll find much guidance there; the publication, and others like it, focuses mostly on newer automobiles. Instead, use Google to search for past reviews by publications like *Car and Driver*, *Road & Track*, *Hagerty*, and *MotorTrend*. There are other online resources too, like Motorbiscuit, Jalopnik, marque-specific club literature, and the comments section of Bring-a-Trailer, arguably the most popular online auction site on the planet.

In fact, just for fun, let's take an imaginary peek over Ms. Aniston's shoulder in 1994 (the year *Friends* began its decade-long run) and see what she could have learned from today's online resources *before* she forked over $13,000 plus beaucoup bucks in repair bills. In a detailed 2018 review of the Mercedes 280 SL, Classiccars4sale.com, a British website, called the car "the most common, most sought after, and most valuable of all the Pagodas [the name given to Stuttgart's series of sports cars that began with the 230 SL in 1963]." And that was just for starters. The website quoted another reviewer, who exulted, "No one could have anything but the highest praise for the magnificent seats, driving position and visibility, the impeccable finish, one of the best power steering systems there is, and roadholding that must be as safe as any other production car in the world."

Wow. What could go wrong, right? A lot, as it turns out. Classiccars4sale ticked off a few watch-out-for particulars:

ENGINE TROUBLE: Though the cast-iron bottom is Mercedes-bulletproof, the aluminum cylinder head can fall victim to corrosion, especially in the absence of appropriate levels of antifreeze. Watch the temperature gauge on start-up; if it quickly heads too far north, the radiator may be clogged. Not surprisingly, the best medicine for long engine life are 3,000-mile 20W/50 oil changes; dirty oil can lead to camshaft wear and fuel pump damage.

BODY/CHASSIS: Keep a watchful eye for rust and corrosion. Get underneath the car to check floor pans and especially foot cavities, bumper mountings, and rear chassis members. Don't skip front body panels around headlights and wheel arches.

DRIVETRAIN: Classiccars4sale rates the Pagoda auto trannies as "forever" parts unless fluid levels are allowed to drop. Power steering box is similarly reliable as long as it isn't leaking, and suspension is long-lived as long as it gets a good greasing every 3,000 miles.

The PPI: An *always* 'to do'

In July 2021, a 280 SL brought $72,700 on Bring-a-Trailer.com, and the car and its sale were instructive. The seller had owned the vehicle for nineteen years and in that time had painstakingly refurbished—though not restored—the car from bumper to bumper. The original silver paint had been stripped and the body repainted in a dazzling Signal Red. The existing engine was replaced by a rebuilt I-6 from a 280 SE coupe. The transmission, brakes, power steering, floor pans, wiring, fuel system, and windshield had been replaced. The interior had been refinished, including fresh parchment MB-Tex seats (though without original headrests); the familiar Mercedes steering wheel had given way to a varnished-walnut replacement by Nardi. In short, the car was drivable on a daily basis—in effect, a near-new 1968 280 SL.

However, because of its many alterations, the pretty sportster no longer could be called original. As one BaT commentator put it, "Being a 'bitsa' [car with bits and pieces from many others] it will never be a Concours car. Many who buy cars to drive will be perfectly happy with this car; those who buy cars for show will move on." That said, however, it might have been the perfect purchase for Ms. Aniston, who fell in love with the 280 SL's looks and asked only that it take her home. Best of all, in 1994 dollars it would have cost only $39,000—extra money she may well have spent anyway in repairs.

Which, of course, goes back to our first proscription. Know what you want to use the car for.

Hank Johnson, a Phoenix, Arizona, collector who has been buying and selling cars for years, offers this prepurchase advice: "Research, research, research." A first-time buyer can never

know too much; many foibles are unique to particular years and models.

"Even legendary cars have gremlins in certain years," says Johnson. "As an example, I bought a '71 Porsche 911-T. It was a beautiful car, but what I didn't know was that for that year and model Porsche cheapened down on the carbs from Webers to Solexes. They were notorious for catching fire, and mine did so twice, with major engine compartment damage, wiring harnesses, air cleaners, paint, on and on. I fixed it the first time and it did it again."

Do your homework, Johnson advises. Know the pitfalls of given model years and marques. And study values based on the relative condition of the make, year, and model. Hagerty, for example, offers free online valuation tools that rank vintage cars in price bands based on condition—Concours (Best-in-World), Excellent, Good, and Fair. Hagerty and sites like Classic. com track auction sales and generate realistic profiles of what cars are actually worth. Vintage automobile values experience ups and down like any other investment; a new buyer needs to know where they stand at any given time in the market.

Most importantly—if only he had spoken to Ms. Aniston—Hank urges a newbie purchaser to determine as accurately as possible the full potential costs to bring the vehicle "to the standard you aspire to—then add at least 25 percent." Warning: Often those expenses will eclipse the original price. Some other Hank tips:

1. Hire a qualified pro, preferably an expert in the marque, to perform a PPI—a prepurchase inspection. If the seller is reluctant to allow this, walk.

2. The PPI will most likely cover the car's drivetrain and mechanical components. But don't overlook other potential costs. Consider a magnet test to determine the quality of the car's cosmetics. Or carry a hardware store magnet to detect suspect areas, especially on fenders and front and rear ends. "Bondo, a decent body person, and flashy paint can disguise a lot of very costly sins," warns Hank, "not to mention safety issues of structural integrity. Cars can appear to be unbelievably beautiful when, up close, they aren't."

The ultimate answer: try to personally view and test-drive any car you are seriously considering. Pros like Hank often talk about "20-foot cars" and "10-foot cars" and even "5-foot cars" to describe vehicles that look great at a short distance but disappoint the closer you get. This is especially true in the era of online purchases of vintage vehicles—transactions that were rare only a few years ago. If you can't see and drive the car yourself, consider the PPI and other expert analysis even more important.

Compile an accurate history of the car, from its initial owner to the present day. Your author has the first buyer's operating manual for a vintage Mercedes he purchased a few years ago. The booklet is contained in its original clear plastic cover that includes a holder for the first buyer's business card (he was a haberdasher in the Midwest, purchased the car new, and owned it until his death in 2016). A more likely scenario is that your car has had several owners—you should identify them all. Find out how the car was maintained and kept. Are there complete service records? Was the car garaged? By all its owners?

Many manufacturers can provide letters of authenticity and "build sheets," which Hank Johnson regards as a birth certificate for your investment. These can include the date and

Check shutlines: chipless and seamless is best

location of final assembly, original paint codes, engine type, factory options such as alloy wheels, and the vehicle's ultimate destination for sale. Most marques will provide these letters for a fee, though simple build sheets may be obtained at little or no charge.

Though perhaps not of compelling interest to most NextGen buyers, European automakers increasingly offer formal authentication services for especially valuable vintage models. Launched in 2006, for example, Ferrari Classiche certifies the authenticity of a car's heritage and validates—and may insist on carrying out—any and all repairs, parts, and bodywork to correct previous lapses from originality. Some may resent the service, which can be expensive and heavy-handed and even require shipping the vehicle to the prancing horse factory in Modena. Arguably, however, the process can add to a vintage Ferrari's ultimate resale value. As a final step, the car's owner receives the vehicle's historically accurate service log and a "red book" formally attesting to its authenticity.

Short of going to such esoteric lengths, however, there are many clues that NextGen buyers can detect with their own eyes.

1. Is the car being sold with a dealer's warranty or "as is"? The latter case will apply to nearly all vintage cars, but if you are buying from a dealer, it never hurts to ask.

2. Wear work clothes and inspect the car in daylight when the engine is cool.

3. Check "shut lines" of doors, trunk lids, and bonnets. Are the gaps tight and consistent? Open the doors—do they sag or hang straight and close properly? Look for paint blisters and rust. Keep your magnet handy if you think areas have been filled and/or repainted. As described earlier, crawl under the car and look for rust. Ditto in the car's trunk, a favorite gathering place for rainwater and corrosion.

4. Make sure the vehicle is parked on level ground. Is it sitting evenly? Push down on

the fenders at all four corners. Does it spring back in a single rebound? Grab the tires and pull back and forth. There shouldn't be any movement. Check the tires themselves; wear should be even on all tires, across the tread. Put a penny into the tread with Lincoln's head upside down; if the top of his head is showing, the car needs new tires. A careful buyer can also check the tire's date code (the last four digits after the letters "DOT" show the week and year it was made—tires over six years old should be replaced.)

5. Check the interior. Look for stains, rips, and tears. Are the radio, gauges, and lights all working? Examine the rubber pedal pads— clutch, brake, gas—be aware that spanking fresh pedal pads could indicate the owner is disguising previous heavy use.

6. Lift the hood (first make sure the engine is cool). Remove the radiator cap and look for droplets of oil in the water—a possible sign of deteriorating gaskets. Feel the hoses; they should be flexible. Check battery lugs and cables for corrosion and tightness (loose connections can trigger maddening intermittent starting problems). Pull out the dipstick and examine the oil. Is the oil maple colored? Rub the oil between your fingers; it should feel slippery but not gritty.

7. Look under the vehicle for puddles. They could be oil, water, or other liquids such as a transmission fluid, none of which are good signs.

8. Finally, realize that none of these steps negate the need for a PPI by a qualified mechanic who knows your dream car's marque. Check Yelp and the Better Business Bureau to ensure that the shop you've selected has a good reputation. Study model knowledgeable commenters on Bring-a-Trailer.com. Best of all, get a recommendation from someone who already owns the car you're considering. Any prepurchase inspection should include a compression test of the engine and safety checks of the steering and brakes. Ask for a written report that itemizes any problems needing immediate attention and an estimated cost of addressing them.

Of course, buying your first classic begins with finding a car you want to buy. Online sources like eBay, Bring-a-Trailer, Craigslist, Cars & Bids, and others are obvious starting— and perhaps ending—points, but other possibilities include estate sales and local newspaper ads, or, as did Jennifer Aniston, you might spot a car with a "For Sale" sign on the street. Another source of lore among veteran collectors is the so-called, much-ballyhooed-seldom-experienced-ever-ubiquitous "barn find." Hagerty Media's Tom Cotter has made a career out of turning up neglected treasures in storage buildings, warehouses, long-closed garages and, yes, barns too. "We find Cobras

and Ferraris and I get excited about those," Cotter said in episode 70 of his popular YouTube *Barn Find Hunter* show. "But we find VW pickups and I get excited about those too. The antique hobby movement is going in this direction for young enthusiasts."

Cotter travels 1,000 miles a week searching for abandoned automotive treasures. In that same 70th episode, he enthused over 44 cars that had been gathered over a lifetime by a late collector in rural Reedville, Virginia. Among the dusty, sometimes rusty rides: a completely original 1960 Porsche 1600; a Mercedes 280 SL with 55,000 miles and an ultra rare 4-speed transmission; and a 1952 MG TD boasting a Chevy V-8 with a four-barrel carburetor. Mr. Cotter waxed lovingly over each one, but a 1984 Volkswagen GTI in original condition attracted special attention. "This is the car that changed America's opinion of what a muscle car could be," he said. "It was one of the first pocket rockets."

Treads: See as little of Honest Abe as possible

Lift bonnet, hope for no surprises

In his 2011 article "Confessions of a (Former) Barn Finder" for *The Blitz*, the Opel Motorsport Club magazine, auto writer Wallace A. Wyss offered tips for budding barnies. They included making friends with vintage-car mechanics, most of whom spend at least part of their time fixing up classic cars that are about to be offered for sale; using car club yearbooks to track down inactive members who may have gone into retirement and taken their cars with them (Wyss tells of one collector who hired a private detective to trace an inactive club member who kept a rare Ferrari hidden under a tarp); and cruising wealthy neighborhoods.

Another approach to buying vintage automobiles is fractional ownership. With one such firm, investors purchase shares in collector cars to "flip" or "hold." "Flip" cars offer $100 shares in cars that are held for ninety days or less until they are sold; investors share the financial results—good or bad—with the seller. "Hold" ownership entitles owners of at least 10 percent of fully funded cars to take possession of the vehicle for up to a month. Sixty-five percent of owners must agree to any sale—or they may counteroffer.

Though stretched-thin holders of multi car collections may find such fractional ownership and quick-turnaround investments of interest, we suspect they will not appeal to NextGen buyers searching for a vintage vehicle they can treasure and enjoy, perhaps for years.

Alternatives to fractional ownership schemes include straight-ahead classic car rentals, such as Hank Johnson's Phoenix, Arizona–based Johnson American Driving Experience, findable at JADEaz.com. Current rental sports cars available for a day, a week, or more include Porsches, Aston Martins, Morgans, and Triumphs. Though a marriage certificate is not required, Hagerty's DriveShare can put a honeymooning couple behind the wheel of a 1955 Rolls-Royce Silver Dawn for $700 a day; a 1989 Porsche for $195 per diem; or a Mercedes-Benz 280 SL like Ms. Aniston's for $495. DriveShare renters connect directly with participating owners to ask questions and arrange for pick-up times and locations and the vehicle's return when the rental period is over. Hagerty even has a DriveShare app for mobile phones.

As the reader has probably guessed by now, though he holds nothing against buying, selling, renting, or even fractionally owning classic cars, your author believes there is much to be gained, especially by someone new to the hobby, through a strong association with a single car or marque, one that can impart a depth of knowledge over time, thereby adding years to your enjoyment. He even suspects that, on some cosmic level, having experienced too many "quickie" relationships with vintage cars may equate to having experienced too many

separate relationships with life partners. Please understand these comments do not extend to legitimate collectors, and/or collectible vehicle dealers and auctioneers, without whom there would be no classic car marketplace.

Speaking of legitimacy, any first-time NextGen buyer must be alert to scam artists who lurk on the edges of the collector-car hobby. As Hank Johnson cautions, there are many schemes in the naked city—deals where the unknowing buyer pays shipping fees up front only to learn there is no car, or no title, or the car is frozen in the meat locker of impound. Another Johnson "watch-out-for": the "white knight scheme" where the buyer is left to deal with a stand-in "friend" or "intermediary" while the owner is unreachable at a remote location.

Barn finding can be fun.

Summing up, be super wary of cars that can't be inspected, cars whose owners can't be reached, cars that have been standing still or in long-term storage, or cars whose prices are suspiciously low.

"Spending too much for a really good used car is the best investment you'll ever make," says Keith Martin, founder and publisher of *Sports Car Market* magazine. "You can't make a $15,000 car into a $25,000 car by spending $10,000," he told *The Star*, the Mercedes Car Club of America's official magazine. "We live in an era where there are a lot of undamaged cars available, so why would you ever buy one that didn't have a clear CarFax? Manufacturers can now offer certified pre-owned cars with a warranty because the cars are so good."

As Martin himself admits, however, unlike specimens from the 1980s and '90s, finding vintage cars from the 1960s and '70s is a greater challenge; they came from an era when 50,000 miles on the odometer did not necessarily mean the vehicle possessed another 50,000 miles of trouble-free performance. Hagerty suggests a critical step for pre-1980s cars is to use the VIN decoder at Hagerty.com/apps/valuation tools/search/auto. "We've seen it all," says veteran collector and Hagerty contributor Colin Comer. He cites examples of doctored CarFax reports, changed mileage, and missing repair history. "All it takes is a printer, a pair of scissors, and questionable creativity."

Comer urges online buyers to request emailed high-res photos (at least 800 KB each) so that images can be enlarged and examined in detail.

Wanna rent instead of buy?

Supplement to Sports Car Market

Keith Martin's
Sports Car Market
The Insider's Guide to Collecting, Investing, Values and Trends

THE 2022
POCKET PRICE GUIDE

26th
ANNUAL EDITION

Essential Information You Need to Know!
- Over 2,000 Up-to-Date Prices
- Includes Sports, Classics & Muscle Cars

For SCM Members Only. Not for Sale.

photographs make it onto the transport truck.

Keith Martin remembers seeing a Mercedes 500 SL for sale online and asking about its condition. "The seller said it was good, except for the salvage title, but she added, 'For some extra money I could get you a different title.'" (NextGen buyers should avoid salvage title cars like the proverbial plague—they may be unsafe and extremely difficult to sell or insure.)

"At each layer," Martin concludes, "you drill down to a lower level of assurance, but maybe a better deal. It's like walking through the dark using your checkbook as a flashlight."

Fortunately, our featured collector has moved beyond such concerns. According to recent reports, Ms. Aniston's current automotive stable includes a 2019 Range Rover, a newish Bentley Continental GT, and a 2007 Toyota Prius (the latter vehicle having been recommended for purchase by her neighbor, Leonardo DiCaprio).

These pictures should include known problem areas and defects, even small ones. Comer is also a fan of ride-along videos—they're difficult to alter—that include hot and cold starts. Final purchase arrangements should include a partial payment with the remainder conditioned on a successful PPI and verification of an official title bearing the seller's (or their company's) name. Finally, determine what spare parts, literature, repair records, etc. are included in the sale— and that all parts shown on the car in videos and

9

HOW TO LOVE (AND LIVE WITH) YOUR CLASSIC CAR

"That's the magic of 'unreliable' old cars; they have so much character. It makes repairing them more than replacing parts. It feels like looking after a sick family member or helping a friend."

António Almeida, posting on DriveTribe.com

"**A** classic car has character, personality; it has human qualities," writes Almeida, a self-described "petrolhead" living in Portugal. He compares today's affinity for classic cars to musicians and photographers who've returned to the artistic honesty of analog tape recorders and film cameras. "In a world focused on disposable consumption and instant gratification," Almeida adds ruefully, "most people do not understand this point of view."

We do. But could we—dare we—use the word *love* to help Mr. Almeida clarify his meaning? Put another way, what other emotion could explain the deep connections we have to our classic cars?

How else would we describe the feelings Neil Andrew has for the 1966 Mercedes he's restored over a period of five decades with his dad Gary, a retired Army colonel? The elder Andrew fell for the Silver Star in the 1960s and '70s when he and wife Joann were first stationed in Germany. In 1978, after a string of models, Gary purchased a rusty-but-beautiful 230 SL Pagoda sports car for $4,625.

"Dad began keeping records right away," Neil recounted in "Honor Thy Father," a 2021 article for *The Star*, the Mercedes Club of America magazine. His father began a journal titled, "History of my new car, a 1966 Mercedes-Benz 230 SL, September, 1978."

Thus launched a nearly half-century-long father-son automotive relationship that began with repair and restoration of the car's rusted wheel wells and underbody. The job—which included reinforcing the car's frame and returning its color to the original white body and navy blue hardtop—required 804 hours of labor and the help of a local mechanic. By the early '90s the Andrews—and their now-restored 230 SL—had settled in Alabama. Neil remembered, "The first time I was able to drive the car alone was when I took it to my high school prom in 1994. That evening I felt like the coolest kid alive."

Two years later, the 230 was badly dinged in a parking lot and the family's regular use fell off. Then it stopped altogether; the car sat for twenty-five years. Neil and his dad resolved to restore the car, but, in the interim, Gary Andrew had changed. In 2020, after showing serious signs of dementia, he failed a driving test and lost his license. Neil assured Gary they could still work on the car together and that he and Joann would take him on rides wherever and whenever he wanted to go. As his father's condition worsened, Neil did most of the work to get the Mercedes back in shape. At last, the two men washed and waxed the car and took it in for a professional photo session. They still go on weekend outings and, on one such drive, the odometer clicked past 99,999 kilometers. "I think our 230 SL is ready for a new set of adventures," Neil said, turning to his dad in the seat beside him.

"This car we love ended up giving my father and me quality time together that we would not otherwise have had," Neil concluded. "I feel blessed to have not only restored the SL with him but also to have gained the knowledge he had about this wonderful automobile. We rebuilt the car and our relationship at the same time." In dedicating his article, Neil wrote, "with love and appreciation for my dad, Gary F. Andrew, who has taught me so much about fixing both cars and life."

Classic cars not only appeal to us emotionally, visually, and viscerally, they also strengthen the ties that bind us to our families and, indeed, to the family of man. In his posting, Mr. Almeida celebrated the global impact of England's Land Rover, "the vehicle that discovered the forgotten corners of the planet . . . the only car the most isolated tribes ever saw." Small wonder that he called the rugged, snorkel-breathing, river-

fording vehicles "a piece of automotive history."

His own history propelled Leon K. Humble on a search for the Ford Model T his grandfather, one Carl Maute, bought new in 1918. "It came to his home in North Dakota on a railroad, packed in five or six crates," Mr. Humble, a retired electrical engineer now in his eighties, recalled in a *Wall Street Journal* article by A. J. Baime. "The crates were loaded onto a horse-

Leon Humble on Restoring Grandpa's Model T: "The car that put the world on wheels."

drawn wagon and taken to his farm in Wolford, where he assembled the vehicle himself." Around 1930, Mr. Maute cut the back seats out with a hacksaw and refashioned the car as a pickup truck with a wooden bed.

Mr. Humble's memories include sitting on the T's hood as a four-year-old, driving around the farm in the rain, and getting stuck in the area's dirt roads. Years later, he decided to try and find the old car. It turned out his grandfather, who died in 1951, first loaned the car to a museum, then sold it for $1. In 1996, Mr. Humble tracked down the "new" owner and bought the ancient Ford back, but it was in desperate shape. Unable to start the restoration until 2009, he worked weekends and turned to a local Model T expert for help.

Finishing the job three years later, he has since collected prizes at car shows and driven in numerous parades. "Top speed is 30 to 35 miles per hour," said Mr. Humble. "The Model T [of which Ford built more than 15 million examples between 1908 and 1927] is arguably the most important car ever built. When I think about my childhood memories of this car—and how tough it was—and I think about how much I enjoy driving it now, I can understand why this little model is the one that put the world on wheels."

"I love cars, all cars. Period," says Laura Foster, of Phoenix, Arizona. "When I was a little girl, I chose Hot Wheels over Bambi." In her teens, she learned about auto mechanics from her older brother Billy and by seventeen had saved up enough for a 1969 Chevy Nova. "I wanted a Chevelle but I couldn't afford it," she recalls. Now in her fifties, she met her current husband, a local businessman, at a car show. After they were married, he told her to look in the driveway. "If you like it, it's yours," he said, opening the door to reveal a 1974 maroon Corvette Sting Ray Convertible. "I've loved him like crazy ever since," says Laura.

Since then, she's owned a series of Mustangs, culminating in the 2015 twin-turbo black-and-purple model she calls "Spooky." "Women and kids flock to us," says Laura. "The kids yell, 'Mom, it's a Hot Wheels car! And Spooky shows the ladies it's okay to dress up a car. I think of her as a macho Mustang with a woman's touch." In fact, Laura has a mission: "I want to see women and kids get into cars," she says.

Like not a few Hollywood beauties, Spooky is anything but original. She's had, as they say in celebrity circles, "work done." This includes, but is not necessarily limited to, sparkling rhinestone "bling" inside and splashy vinyl graphics on her exterior. Billet aluminum lug

nuts accentuate her wheels and carbon fiber highlights her 5.0-liter engine. Lamborghini-style "scissor" doors complete the car's major mods, though Laura herself often infuses her tresses with Spooky-matching purple strands. As a final step, she coated her garage floor with a showroom finish. "I knew I'd be down there crawling around," Laura explains, "and I *hate* a dirty garage."

Renée Brinkerhoff didn't begin racing her 356 Porsche out of love. She did it because she had no choice. But it's inspiring—and sweet— how the whole thing ended up.

"I was in my mid-fifties," she told a first-ever Women's Forum titled "Women Who Love Their Cars" at California's Pebble Beach Concours d'Elegance in 2021. She'd had a modified VW

Renee Brinkerhoff: fighting human trafficking in her 356.

Bug at seventeen and remained slightly car crazed ever since. "I'd been saying to myself for decades, 'One day I'm going to race a car!' So I got into it because I had to."

Waiting until the last of her four children left for college, and after training with professional race instructors and sharing some practice runs, Ms. Brinkerhoff chose Mexico's challenging La Carrera Panamericana for her 2013 debut. The 2,000-mile, six-day event's hallmark: long runs of flat-out racing over closed roads. "Whereas mandatory safety features inside the cars have dramatically improved," wrote one participant, competing still requires "steel nerves" and many sections "are today as dangerous as ever."

"I was shaking all over," Ms. Brinkerhoff told her Women's Forum audience of her initial run. "It was a combination of fear of the unknown and fear of failure." Pushing through her doubts and trembles, she became La Carrera Panamericana's first female competitor to win her class.

Beneath its classic skin, her Porsche 356 A has been modified to include a 2-liter boxer engine with Weber carbs, 911 rear suspension, five-speed manual transmission, roll cage, disc brakes at all corners, and a 21-gallon fuel cell. Ms. Brinkerhoff formed Valkyrie Racing—named after the female warriors of Norse mythology—and went on to place in two more Panamericana races. Then she led Valkyrie in launching the Project 356 World Rally Tour. It's mission: to campaign their car on all seven continents, choosing the most challenging rallies on each, with the goal of raising funds to combat child trafficking.

Thus far Ms. Brinkerhoff and her team have competed in seventeen countries on six continents, including the ultra difficult East African Safari Classic across Kenya and Tanzania, raising more than $200,000 for her cause. "The memories of the children around the world that we have been blessed to touch and their innocent faces will forever be in our minds and hearts," she told the *New York Times* in August 2020. Valkyrie's final planned event is to race the Porsche solo over 356 miles of ice in Antarctica, and to score a world speed record on that continent's infamous clear blue ice.

"Racing forced me out of my comfort zone," Ms. Brinkerhoff told the forum attendees. "I got into it because I had to. I stayed in it because I wanted to."

Careful NextGen readers should note that—by no accident—none of the car lovers we've just described could remotely be called kids. So what's the message here? Buy a classic car when you're still in Z, millennial, or Gen X territory and you can hang there, maybe not forever, but longer. Or at least it will *seem* longer. As a bonus, you'll smile more and, as the years go by, those wrinkles around your neck and that meniscus tear you picked up road biking will bother you a lot less.

Car Love: Some Snapshots:

"Only a few New Year's Eves away from turning ninety, I had never owned a Porsche," observed BaT bidder "drcharles2," in a 2021 Auction Success Story. "I didn't know what a 'croc' [Porscheese for 'Cayman,' itself a misspelled reference to the Caiman alligator] was." On September 2, 2020, the doc defeated his BaT competitors to win a 2006 Cobalt Blue Porsche Cayman S, ultra clean and showing just 10,000 miles, for $36,000. "Now is the time," he declared. "You only live once."

Garth Stein's family and friends made fun of him when he bought a 1974 Alfa Romeo GTV, "like I was having another midlife crisis," *The Art of Racing in the Rain* author told the *Wall Street Journal*. The entire time he was drafting the novel, Stein, in his late fifties, had a die-cast miniature GTV on his desk; when finished, he bought the big boy model. "What I love about this car is that it has no computers," Mr. Stein said. "Unlike cars of today, which constantly overload you with information about themselves, this one tells me nothing except what I can experience through my senses—the smells and sounds and such. Every time I drive it is an adventure. There is no power steering; it can be a handful. But I love it like a brother."

Every weekday for forty-five years, Frankie Melder drove "Bess," her stick-shift Corvette hardtop, to her job as a physical therapist in Austin, Texas. "It's a hard thing to let her go," said Ms. Melder upon deciding to list the car on Bring-a-Trailer. "I just hope someone has as much fun and love with this girl as I have. She's a sweetheart." The all-original, matching numbers Corvette sold for $77,777 on November 16, 2017. A month later, Ms. Melder took delivery on a brand-new Porsche 911 Carrera. She was eighty-five years old. "You're my kind of babe!" exclaimed one BaT commenter.

"We weren't really looking for a new car," New York's E. J. Boyd told *The Star* magazine. "But at age eighty-two, my mother suddenly decided she wanted a new convertible to go with her 1972 Mercedes-Benz 280 SE 4.5. In years past, my mother had enjoyed her time owning a 1961 300 SL roadster; guided by her memories of that wonderful automotive experience, her search for a new open-topped Mercedes-Benz began." It ended with a 1985 380 SL, Mr. Boyd reported, and "love at first sight."

So, being a lover of classic cars will keep you young, right? Well, maybe. But as any relationship counselor will tell you, it's one thing to fall in love; the real question is will it last? Or, put more simply, how do you *live* together?

First and foremost, you *must* drive your classic. As Neil and Gary Andrew learned to their dismay, lack of movement is the surest way to damage any car, classic or otherwise. "Often,

I get asked to 'wake up' sitting cars," says car guru and master restorer Wayne Carini. "The big question is, 'How far do you go?' My rule is . . . the car has to run, move, stop, and pass a thorough safety inspection." After that, he is typically asked, "What's the next step?" Once he responds with an estimate for bodywork, paint, and attendant refurbishment of chrome, glass, rubber, and interior—i.e., a full-on restoration—clients often blanche and decide they just want to drive the car.

The recipe for avoiding these scenarios begins with carefully choosing the right car in the first place. When buying a car, assess its cosmetic needs—they will often be more costly to address than mechanical issues. As suggested in the previous chapter, look closely for signs of the dreaded tin worm—rust. And remember what has become the holy grail of collectors: originality. In the past, this wasn't true. Cars were frequently restored to a level that exceeded their condition when new. Today's choosiest collectors, however, utter a now-familiar mantra: "A car is only original once." Your goal should be to keep it that way, at least as much as possible (some true-life exceptions noted below).

Also, repeating previous advice, know the pitfalls of your car's particular year, model, and marque. To cite an example, it's fortunate that Mr. Boyd's mom chose a 1985 model 380 SL. That's because beginning the year before, Stuttgart fitted the 380 with a double-row timing chain; in earlier years' models, single-row chains had a disturbing tendency to snap, causing grievous engine damage. By contrast, the two-row chains, according to *The Star*, "allowed these engines to reliably endure hundreds of thousands of miles." Anti lock brakes were another welcome improvement in 1985, along with improved headrests, a smaller safety steering wheel, and an aluminum hood.

Glenn Oliveria, who for more than four decades has serviced, rebuilt, and maintained

Frankie Melder's 'Bess': a 45-year love affair.

vintage cars, especially Alfa Romeos and Ferraris, at his shop in Berkeley, California, recommends that new owners thoroughly educate themselves about their cars. Obtain original (or copies thereof) owner's, shop, and parts manuals. These may be available online for purchase or printing, from your marque's car club or association, or from specialty book sellers. "Part of the fun of having an old car is learning about it," says Oliveria . Resources like parts manuals can help NextGen buyers learn and list what's needed to restore or retain their vehicle's originality, he adds.

Mr. Oliveria purpose-built his airy shop, with its sturdy concrete-block walls and skylight ceilings, from the ground up. A professionally trained mechanical engineer, as sole proprietor of Oliveria Engineering, he employs the problem-solving methodology of an engineer in addressing customers' automotive issues, leavened with decades of experience.

His respect for originality approaches the devotional, yet he is open to deviation if it offers improved performance or reliability or, hopefully, both.

A case is point is offered by the author's own long-cherished 1964 Alfa Romeo Spider 2600. Coachbuilt by Touring, the relatively rare Spider came with three stock Solex carburetors. Though the Solexes were original equipment, most enthusiasts prefer Weber carbs, which offer significantly improved performance. Mr. Oliveria agreed to install Webers on the 2600 but wisely insisted on using carbs with a throttle opening 5 millimeters narrower than the more commonly employed 45-millimeter version. The payoff for his marque-deep knowledge and years of experience: miles of motoring enjoyment without Solex issues of burned valves or 45-millimeter Weber issues of finicky tuning.

The above example illustrates perhaps the most important lesson of all in showing your love for your car: finding a gifted and knowledgeable mechanic.

However, that still leaves plenty of tasks for you, the new owner. Here are a few suggestions:

1. Purchase a *fitted* car cover. This is always your author's first step in acquiring a "new" old car. That's because nothing is more important in terms of protecting your vehicle inside as well as out. Sun, rain, snow, hail, pets, pests, and people are just some of the enemies that can harm your car's paint finish and interior, especially leather upholstery. Oh sure, you can just toss an old blanket or comforter over your vehicle in the garage, but outside it could blow away in a stiff breeze and inside it may slip out of place. Some caveats: look for a cover with "ears," i.e., pockets for your car's exterior mirrors. And insist on a "breathable" cover that allows any moisture that gets under the

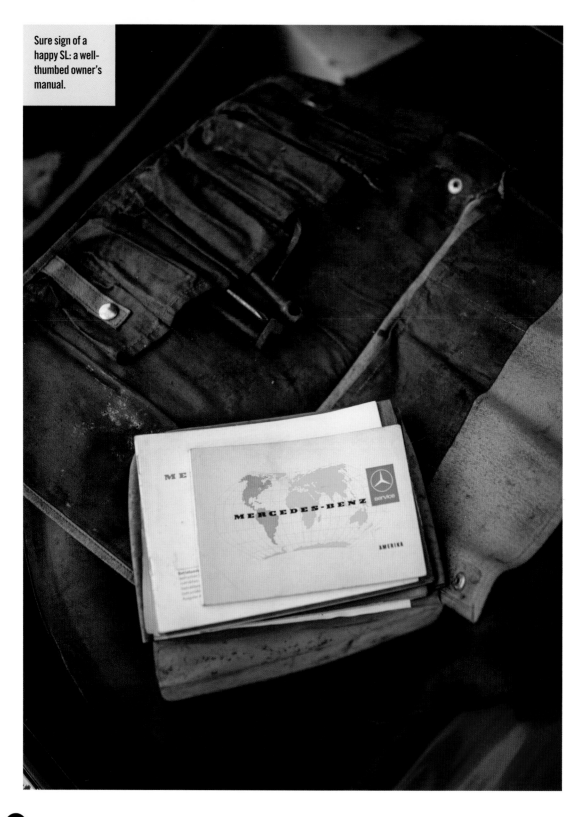

surface to evaporate. Be sure to choose a cover designed specifically for your car, rather than a cheaper "universal-fit" model that may slip or move around. Let your cover air dry if it has been out in the rain; covers may contain synthetic materials that can be damaged in a household dryer.

2. Touch your car like you would a lover. That means wash the finish, wax it, seal it. And don't wash the car with plain tap water and dishwasher soap. Proper car shampoos contain gentle lubricants so dust and grime don't abrade the surface. These aren't hard to find—check out brands like Meguiar's Gold Class Shampoo and Conditioner or similar products from Griot's Garage, Turtle Wax, Adam's Polishes, and countless others. You might even try Rain-X waterless spray in areas of drought or limited water availability. When it comes

to wax, we generally avoid cutting polishes unless necessary and, when they are, we prefer Klasse All-in-One, which gently removes old wax, minor swirls, and oxidation and leaves a protective coating. "I have used this product for years and it is still my all-in-one product," wrote one five-star reviewer. "Yes, I may finish with another product, BUT start with this first." Good advice. The careful car lover will follow with a wax such as P21S Concours Carnauba Wax, Wolfgang Deep Gloss Paint Sealant, or any of a number of similar wax-only products from Meguiar's, Mothers, or other manufacturers. Always use a soft foam applicator and finish with a microfiber towel. Finally, consider one of the new ceramic sealants, like Radiant, from Jay

Always cover when not in use.

Leno's Garage, or similar products from Griot's Garage, Autogeek, and others. And don't forget those polymer-based quickie detailers such as P&S's excellent Bead Maker Paint Protectant, Meguiar's Ultimate Quik Detailer and Quik Wax, etc., for in-between freshenings.

3. Always stock color-correct touch-up paint in your garage. These are available from manufacturers like Dr. ColorChip and on websites such as Autogeek.net. You'll need the make, model, and year of your car or its color code, the latter of which should be listed on

Even a Ferrari 458 needs a loving touch.

your car's build sheet. Fine brushes are good to have as well as lacquer thinner for cleanup. This is one of those items to keep on hand for those inevitable minor nicks and chips.

4. Use the correct fluids. Gasoline is easy; pump what's right for your car. Most of the vehicles we've talked about in this NextGen guide will be happiest running on 90+ octane fuels, typically called Premium, Supreme, etc., or, in the very olden days, Ethyl. Motor oil is more complicated. Check out oils like Lucas Hot Rod & Classic or Castrol GTX Classic; both contain zinc and/or phosphorous formulations that can prolong the life of cams and tappets BUT should not be used with cars that have

catalytic converters. To drive yourself crazy on this subject, head over to Bobistheoilguy.com, where you'll learn more about oil than you ever wanted to know.

5. Another mental playground for NextGen car buyers: the gazillions of goops, concoctions, and secret potions available from additives makers. Among the oldest of these, 100 year old Marvel Mystery Oil is said to enhance performance and extend engine life; it can be added to the crankcase, the gas tank, or both—just follow directions. Lucas, Red Line, STP, Gumout, and Chevron's venerable Techron are just a few of the multitudinous fuel injector and carburetor cleaners on the market; many contain polyetheramine (PEA) detergents, said to be a superior remover of engine deposits. Many of the same makers offer other additives they

The best fuel is the right fuel.

say can seal transmission leaks and solve other mechanical issues. Let your trusted mechanic be your guide.

As described in our book's preface, like many before him, loving memories of working with his father drew Gen Xer and Californian Kurt Glaubitz back to the world of classic cars. Now, as did his own dad, Mr. Glaubitz toils alongside his teenage son Cole beneath the bonnet of an aged vehicle whose maker first opened its doors in Warwickshire, England, in 1885. Love radiates between father, son, and the old Land Rover like an electric current. Cole says his girlfriend loves the car too. "She thinks it's really cool," he says, sanding out a rusty rear hatch.

10

FINDING YOUR TRIBE

"Yes, it's about the cars, but in the end, it's the stories, the shared experiences, and the friendships that touch our hearts."

Cindy Banzer, president, Alfa Romeo Owner's Club

"**V**irtually every time the car went out it won," Ferrari restorer Patrick Ottis is telling the assemblage of worshipful Alfa Romeo club members gathered in his shop. He motions toward the gleaming white 1955 750 Monza Spyder occupying center stage on the garage floor. Mr. Ottis quickly sketches the four-cylinder Ferrari's short but illustrious history: driven to victory by future Formula One World Champion and three-time 24-hour Le Mans winner Phil Hill *and* Cobra creator and *Ford v Ferrari* star Carroll Shelby in consecutive 1955 and 1956 Pebble Beach Road Races through California's Del Monte Forest; subsequent winner of successive SCCA races in Louisiana, Texas, and Kansas; key player in daylong battles with famed Sebring stars Mike Hawthorn and Briggs Cunningham in 1954 and

It goes like stink:" Ferrari restorer Patrick Ottis, describing '55 Monza to Alfisti.

'55. Purchased by legendary driver Jim Hall for $7,500 in 1955. Put in a shed and forgotten in 1958. Bought by Mr. Ottis in a 2019 tax exchange involving a prize-winning 1934 Alfa. Now back in action, the nearly seven-decade-old Monza is again being driven successfully by Ottis's NextGen son (the aptly named) Tazio, twenty-six. "It's very predictable and nicely balanced," the elder Ottis says of their car. He smiles slightly. "And it just really goes like stink."

As always, the Alfa club's annual visit to the Ottis family shop is a memorable one. First, it's a chance to hang with and learn about some world-class vehicles from a guy who's crawled in, under, and around some of the best sports cars on the planet. The highly respected Mr. Ottis is a treasure chest of juicy detail, imparting the kind of morsels any cognoscenti can appreciate. He dissects, for example, the important differences between cast and forged pistons; describes

the delicate ergonomics of removing—and preserving—a vintage wiring harness; and compares the gemlike nuts and bolts in a classic Maserati with the brutish—but also brutishly strong—ones in the cars from Maranello.

For the attending Alfisti, however, another big part of the fun is the deepening of connections to their *tribe*; seeing car buddies they haven't talked to since the past summer; catching up on *their* car stories; gossiping about members who aren't in attendance; swapping breakdown sagas; bragging about and bemoaning cars bought and sold. As Theresa Gilpatrick, former executive director of the Ferrari Club of America

of America boast around 4,000 members worldwide. Marque-only clubs account for thousands more. For example, in addition to her lifetime membership in the FCA (currently at a high of 6,700 members), Ms. Gilpatrick belongs to the 10,000-member Audi; 8,000-member BMW; and 100,000-member-and-counting Porsche clubs. "Clubs can help you gain experiences in cars you never would have experienced before," she says, "and you'll meet people you'd have never known before."

Today's car clubs fall into "distinct buckets," Ms. Gilpatrick continues: "Those who have figured out how to engage the next generation and those who have not, for a variety of reasons. The brass and prewar era clubs are struggling to maintain or gain members. Those cars are glamorous and have tremendous history but are nearly impossible to use in modern-day traffic. Parts are often unobtainable. Their members are loyal, but aging, and the numbers are dwindling." For the most part, the marque clubs have figured out how to retain current members and encourage new, younger people; as a result, their numbers are steady or growing.

Ms. Gilpatrick's Skip Barber Racing School plays an active role in that process with NextGen-focused classes in subjects such as learning to shift a manual transmission. Though few have ever experienced stick shifts, "most of our younger students are eager to learn," she says, "and they come out of the training with big smiles. It opens up a whole new world for them." Another Barber course teaches Hagerty Driving Academy survival skills such as accident avoidance, advanced car control, and specific instruction in safe handling—typically taught using '70s American Mustangs and Camaros.

Monterey, California's annual Car Week arguably ranks as the largest of all paeans

and current head of membership development for the Skip Barber Racing School, puts it: "You join a club for the cars, but you stay for the people."

Some 40,000 of those people belong to the Sports Car Club of America; even brass-era groups like the Horseless Carriage Club

A sea of red: Concorso Italiano, the world's largest display of Italian automotive exotica?

to automotive tribalism, at least in America. Tens of thousands of car lovers descend on the forested peninsula each August to attend the Pebble Beach Concours d'Elegance, ranked by many as the world's premier collector car show. Nearby Concorso Italiano is said to be the planet's largest display of Italian cars; Legends of the Autobahn features Mercedes and BMW vehicles; the separate Porsche Monterey Classic is devoted to Porsche cars. Crowds swarm Thursday's Tour d'Elegance, when Pebble Beach entrants line Carmel's Ocean Avenue. Additional shows and events are held in the nearby towns of Pacific Grove and Seaside, and at the Carmel Mission Inn on Rio Road. All the while, hundreds of millions in collectible automobiles change hands during Car Week, both in private treaty transactions and at public auctions.

Meanwhile, younger collectors are forming their own tribal gatherings, such as RADwood events. A growing number of initiatives aim at luring NextGeners into traditional tribe settings. A case in point: a recently launched 30-under-30 class at the annual uber-elegant Audrain Auto Museum concours in Newport, Rhode Island. The brainchild of part-time state resident Jay Leno—honorary chairman at the Audrain show's inauguration—the class is open to entrants up to thirty years old who spend $30,000 or less on their vehicles, including repairs, mods, and/or restoration. "We had a huge turnout and these kids were so excited," Leno said afterward. "Seeing a twenty-six-year-old kid who did all the work in his garage get treated the same way you see a millionaire who had his Bugatti restored in Europe was great. That's the way to grow the hobby."

Enthusiasm ran so high that in its second year—actually held in 2021 due to the pandemic—the 30-under-30 event expanded with a second class, a marque-specific category

devoted to entry-level 944 Porsches built from 1982 to 1991.

"As the entries arrived," said Audrain CEO Donald Osborne, "the event's organizers found themselves saying, 'There's a 944. There's another. There's another.' And suddenly there was a full class of the entry-level Porsches produced from 1982 through 1991."

"The 944 is interesting in that it shows what the true crossover is in collecting." Mr. Osborne told Classiccars.com. "People like myself remember the 944 when it was new and remember the car fondly. And there are young people who are looking for an engaging and interesting driving experience and are looking for a way to get into an iconic marque like Porsche. The 944 appeals to the sixty-year-old and to the twenty-year-old, and for the same reasons—the driving experience."

Equipped with a Porsche-made, liquid-cooled, front-mounted, four-cylinder engine that produced nearly 150 horsepower, the 944 later used turbocharging to boost output above

Cars and Caffeine event at Hagerty's Ann Arbor, MI, office.

240 horses. Despite its complex transmission setup, Mr. Osborne noted, ambitious younger owners who can do their own work are rewarded with a true sports car, one "that can be both a daily driver and a track-day vehicle, as well as qualifying for a major Concours d'Elegance." Indeed, the event was so successful that Mr. Osborne looked forward to featuring a third 30-under-30 class the following year.

So breaking it down, what are some key reasons a NextGen collector should join a car tribe?

1. Inevitably, joining a tribe will enhance and enrich your automotive education. Becoming more sophisticated in the attributes and shortcomings of your chosen marque can serve as the equivalent of a graduate degree in the specific models that have attracted your interest. And fellow club members will almost always be happy to serve as mentors. This can

Mini Mite: a sixties Honda Coupe at Pacific Grove, California's "Little Car Show."

be especially helpful if you are drawn to low-production—that is, rarer—or older cars. In fact, joining a tribe *before* purchasing the car of your dreams can be a smart way of avoiding pitfalls and heartache later on. Ms. Gilpatrick, for example, joined the Porsche club in advance of her anticipated purchase of a Porsche 997.

2. As an active member of your tribe, you will experience cars that would otherwise remain forever unavailable or unattainable. Inevitably, you'll be asked to join someone in their new model or be invited to drive the latest offerings of a given automaker. For example, in 2019, as part of a club demonstration, your author found himself behind the wheel of one of the world's most powerful production cars at that time, a 500-horsepower Alfa Romeo GT sedan. The experience was thrilling if not a little frightening to someone used to the maker's vintage models. Still, it increased his knowledge of the marque and its lineup.

3. You will make lifelong friendships. Car tribe relationships soon morph into social relationships. "You see the same people at Pebble, then at Amelia Island and other shows,

and pretty soon it starts to feel like family," says Ms. Gilpatrick. As one club friend told her son, "I knew you before you were born." Even death itself isn't an insurmountable tribal barrier. When a past Ferrari club president died, Ms. Gilpatrick says she and other members stepped forward to urge his widow to remain active in club activities and events; "we can't see her disappearing," she says.

4. Tribal connections, especially among fellow club members, often become go-to sources for hard-to-find parts and information. Need that adjustable seat rail for your early '60s Alfa Giulietta Sprint? Chances are a fellow member who owns that same coupe has a spare or knows where to find one. As a club member, you'll probably receive an online or print publication—or both—where such "unobtainium" might turn up in a classified ad. The Alfa Romeo 2600 toolkit is worth about $5,000—if you can find one—and original kits for vintage Ferraris can

be valued at $20,000 or more. In addition, tribe-specific dealers such as Moss Motors offer parts and accessories for British-only marques including MG, Triumph, and Austin-Healey. Auto Atlanta provides similar services for air-cooled Porsches, including 356 and 914–6 models.

5. Selling—or buying—a car can be an easier and happier experience if you are dealing with a fellow tribe member. Chances are other members know the vehicle and are familiar with its warts and wows. Thus, it's less likely for either buyer or seller to fudge on a given car's condition or make a painful mistake on pricing. Parts are more readily—and fairly—exchanged, and whichever end of the transaction you are on, odds are you'll know more about whomever you are dealing with. Still, it pays to tread carefully.

Hank Johnson, the Arizona-based collector and enthusiast car rental operator we quoted in an earlier chapter, offers another caveat: tribes change just like people do. "Know your focus of interest before you get involved," he suggests, "but be aware that an organization may change over time and move away from the interest that originally got you involved." In his own case, Mr. Johnson joined the Porsche Club of America because the local region offered training in competitive driving. "I managed to work up to become a competitive regional and International Motor Sports Association (IMSA) driver as well as a high-speed test driver for Lexus," he says. Mr. Johnson became the club's president and together with vice president Margie Smith-Haas (she drove in the 24-hour Le Mans and for Dan Gurney's All American Racers) kept the club's focus on racing. Membership quadrupled.

"We traveled and raced in groups all over Arizona, California, and Nevada, held awards banquets at the end of the year, took club

Carter Kramer and his winning BMW 2002 at Audrain Museum Event for 30-year-olds.

The Porsche 944: a generational crossover in collecting.

drives on the weekends," Mr. Johnson says. "I got the start I wanted out of PCA." But as the membership climbed to over a thousand, the club changed, drifting into more of a social group. Johnson moved on and never looked back.

In fact, the more rarefied one's interest in cars, the more crucial participation in an appropriate tribe turns out to be. "I've always been active in clubs; I can't stress their importance enough," says Chris Paulsen, who teaches restoration skills at Kansas's McPherson College. The former national president of the Horseless Carriage Club of America, Mr. Paulsen inherited his love of so-called "brass era" cars from his father. He's the third generation of his family to own and drive pre-1916 vehicles. "I believe the secret to getting and keeping people

interested in cars is getting them behind the wheel," he says. His daughters "started driving our early cars as soon as they could reach the pedals," Mr. Paulsen reports. "My oldest, now seventeen, just finished restoring her own 1914 Model T Ford."

Mr. Paulsen concedes global membership rolls in clubs devoted to century-old-plus machines may have faded in recent years, but rather than an actual fall-off in interest, he attributes much of the decline to the growing dominance of ubiquitous electronic communications. "It used to be if you needed the latest information on a Model A Ford, you'd have to wait for next month's club magazine to come out," he says. "Now the accessibility of information is instant." Friendships develop online too, and without dues and monthly meetings. "Twenty-five years ago if you were an early car person in the middle of nowhere, you were out there all by yourself. Now the internet reaches everybody, no matter where they are."

Despite acknowledging the positive impact of social media and the internet, Mr. Paulsen is doubtless not alone in preferring the camaraderie of flesh-and-blood tribespeople. "I can't replace the close friends I've made in this hobby," he says. "Some of them I've known since I was a kid. My greatest joy with these early cars is getting out in a group and driving 500 or 600 miles in a week. You really can only get that by being part of a club. Cars bring you together, but the people keep you together," he says, echoing the comments of Ms. Gilpatrick and others.

But car clubs congregate not only near the cold beer on patios or in the nether regions of dusty garages or, for that matter, in the vaporous fringes of the electronic ether. As GQ.com reported in 2019, for tribal members with sufficient resources, exclusive car clubs can and do flourish in cloistered settings steeped in luxury. In an article titled "6 Stylish Car Clubs for the True Enthusiast," the website's Dennis Tang described a new generation of car clubs "that provide a way to wring every drop of performance from your gajillion-horsepower, six- or seven-figure acquisition, all while keeping you in the lap of luxury—when you aren't sweating it out behind the wheel, that is."

Perusing Mr. Tang's list, however, is not for the faint-hearted or tribesfolk on a tight budget. Palm Springs, California's Thermal Club, for example, requires the upfront purchase of an empty lot adjacent to the club's 5.1-mile racetrack. Cheapest lot: $750,000. And that's *before* an initial membership fee of $85,000 and annual dues of $14,400. Of course, one can always exercise the optional purchase of a prebuilt villa at a cool $3 million. Meanwhile, in nearby Arizona, Scottsdale's Otto Car Club offers a stylishly modern, museum-quality garage for collectors who like to look at other people looking at their cars. The lighting is superb, and a billiards room, library, and wet

Unobtainium: an original Alfa Romeo 2600 tool kit.

bar turn Otto into a perfect backdrop for cocktail parties and elegant tribal minglings. Other powwow-perfect places: the Classic Car Club of Manhattan, which offers private instruction and enthusiast cars you can borrow for a spin on nearby roads or its 4.1-mile track; Illinois's Autobahn Country Club, with its comparatively miserly $40,000 initiation and $5,250 annual fees, plus a short but challenging racing circuit and single-day passes; and the Ascari Race Resort in Ronda, Spain, named after famed 1950s Ferrari champion Alberto, which offers its own farmhouse restaurant and helipad.

A tribe has been defined as a community with shared interests that provides mutual support to its members. Tribes exist because humans (and higher animals) are wired at birth for connection, communication, and companionship. Automotive tribes like the ones described in this chapter are no different. Whatever their specific focus and attraction, be it by marque, model, era, or shared venues such as local cars and coffee gatherings, or in the savoring of the freedom of the open road itself, their existence is integral to the full enjoyment of collectible cars—by *all* generations.

11

WHEN AND HOW TO SELL YOUR CLASSIC CAR

$850,000	
£654,500	
€765,000	
SWISS FRANC	824,500

GOODING
&COMPANY

GOODING
&COMPANY

"Yes, I know it sounds stupid, but I cried all afternoon over selling a car. Why, why, why all the tears? Because a car isn't just a car. It is who you are, at least for the moment."

Holly Robinson, novelist and ghost writer, on Huffpost.com

Presale rule: if your car has mechanical problems, fix 'em. If not fixed, disclose 'em.

H olly Robinson's sentiments about parting ways with her daily driver—per her description, a "beat-up" 2003 Honda CRV "with probably enough forgotten food in it to sustain a family of five for a week"—ring even truer when it comes to selling our beloved first classics. Yet, like the approaching clank of some grim automotive reaper, that ominous day inevitably comes.

Part of the reason may be found in the true nature of our relationships with these very special cars. We have chosen them with great care, but usually for more emotional than rational reasons. In all likelihood, they did not, for example, capture our hearts thanks to their miserly fuel consumption, infallible reliability, or their capacity to ferry large numbers of small humans to and from soccer games. No, like some devastating lover, they lured us with their looks, their fine figures, their quirky but irresistible natures, and—as they hurtled down straightaways and deftly rounded the twisties—their unfailing ability to thrill us and send our spirits soaring.

Together, we weathered the bad times too. Indeed, the frustrating—and often embarrassing—occasional tows to mechanics and garages and repair shops only deepened our feelings. And provided rich fodder for future

She's beautiful, now she's ready for a goodbye kiss.

tales of breakdown dramas to be spun and respun (and further embellished) by ourselves and—less enjoyably—others. But somehow, like misbehaving children, each calamity strengthened our ties to the cars we loved and made the severing of those ties when we sold them even more painful to bear. As 60s pop singer Neil Sedaka once sang:

"Think of all that we've been through,
And breaking up is hard to do."

According to a 2013 survey by Autotrader.com, the reason automotive breakups are hard to do is that "our relationships with our cars are surprisingly similar to our relationships with friends." More than 70 percent of respondents felt "very attached" or "somewhat attached" to their cars; a third wore their feelings on their sleeves, describing their conveyance as "an old friend." And more than one in four said thinking about parting ways with the family warhorse made them sad.

As discussed in chapter 9, "How to Love—and Live with—Your Classic Car," a classic car, especially an owner's *first* classic car, can only intensify those feelings. Moreover, as opposed to the family beater—apologies to Ms. Robinson intended—chances are the esteemed car you plan to sell is—or most definitely should be—in better shape than it was when you made your purchase. And therein lies a little discussed complication in owner–classic car relationships. We call it the "I've done everything I can to and for this beauty; now she's somebody else's to love and worry about" syndrome.

Be assured that your author has personally experienced the pain of vehicular divorce. Following are excerpts from a letter he wrote to longtime mechanic and friend Glenn Oliveria, owner of Oliveria Engineering in Berkeley, California.

Dear Glenn:

This is a note to let you know that I am planning to sell my beloved Alfa.

It's been a difficult decision. The 2600 is the favorite of all my Alfas—I've owned it for over twenty years. There's just nothing like that six-cylinder engine: the sound of it; the torque of it; the sheer beauty of its aluminum castings. My memories of the car could fill its big Touring-body trunk. When she was little, Racheal and her friends giggled in the tiny back seat; one night we managed to squeeze in another couple for a quick trip to dinner in Mendocino. I know I'll never match the feeling I get when blasting through the back country in Marin or cruising along the coast.

So my heart says never let it go. But my brain says I must. The car is really at its absolute peak, the best it's ever been. Short of pulling the engine and going into a full restoration— which it doesn't need—there's really no more to be done. So the days of having fun little projects are gone. At the same time, I've gotten increasingly leery of driving it on the street,

'Dear Glenn, I'm planning to sell my beloved Alfa...'

which is something I used to do all the time. Now, knowing there is no traffic enforcement in Oakland and an increasing number of accidents, I only take her out on Sunday mornings, zip around the lake, and tuck her back in the garage as quick as I can. And the increasing value of the car adds another strain: I never wanted a $100K trailer queen. I just wanted a beautiful Alfa I'd love to drive and could afford.

Anyhow, mostly I'm writing this letter to say thank you. Without you Glenn, I could never have owned the 2600 at all. If you hear of any Giulia Supers for sale, let me know.

The point is that human/collector car relationships pass through discernible phases, both in terms of the cars, and in terms of their owners. After years in the real estate business, Mercedes enthusiast and Connecticut resident Winthrop Baum compares these stages to those of home ownership. "In their twenties," he says, his voice assuming a rhythmic pattern, "buyers admire. In their thirties and forties, they acquire. In their fifties they enjoy and expand, showing their cars and participating in rallies and meets. In their sixties, they're still active

but beginning to consolidate. By their seventies and eighties, around the time they're planning to sell the family home, they begin asking, 'What will happen to my beautiful car? Who will take care of it?'"

Mr. Baum, president of the Mercedes-Benz Club of America's Westchester-Connecticut Section, hit upon an unusual idea: a "generational auction," where older owners would sell their cherished made-in-Stuttgart machines to younger purchasers. "Most auctions involve anonymous transactions with cars going to unknown bidders," he says. "I thought, 'Why not create a friendly setting where sellers and buyers from different generations could come together in a comfortable way?'"

Though COVID-related concerns forced postponement of the planned "November to Remember" event in 2021, Mr. Baum's Connecticut club and MBCA's New York City and Northern New Jersey chapters vowed to reschedule the auction in the future.

The proposed sale would differ from typical transactions in which collector cars are sold to anonymous buyers via commercial auction houses, global internet sites, or specialized

Roxie Hendry: 'It was time to let go, but I wanted somebody to love the car as much as I do.'

brick-and-mortar dealers. When an owner passes, larger collections are often broken up because surviving relatives don't share the departed's passion or relish the prospect of maintaining vintage automobiles. In other words, they are *reactive* sales. By contrast, Mr. Baum's planned sale—following a formal black-tie dinner and accompanied by music provided by the Norwalk Symphony Orchestra—would *proactively* unite sellers and buyers and do so when both parties were still alive.

"When I first heard about this I thought, 'What a great idea!'" said Roxie Hendry, of Port St. Lucie, Florida. Ms. Hendry learned of the auction through a Mercedes club bulletin. Her silver metallic 2003 SL 500 had been a gift from her late husband and still showed fewer than 40,000 miles on the odometer. "When I'm sitting in the cockpit, I feel like I'm in an airplane," she says. "It drives like a dream."

Ms. Hendry notes she and her late husband had owned Corvettes and other sports cars—Chuck Hendry's last car was a Mustang Bullitt—over the course of their marriage. "I've always loved speed," she says.

Still, at seventy-eight, she was beginning to experience difficulty getting in and out of the low-slung vehicle as easily as she once had. "It was time to let go," she says, "but I wanted somebody to keep the car and love it as much as I do. At a big commercial auction, it would just go to somebody I'd never meet or know."

Another planned sale participant, age seventy-four, looked forward to offering both his ninety-five-year-old father-in-law's pristine 1983 diesel sedan along with his own ultra clean 1984 500 SEC coupe. Designed by longtime Daimler-Benz styling chief Bruno Sacco, the handsome two-door cost $65,000-plus when new and claimed a top speed of 140 miles per hour. But recently the man's wife asked, "What if something happens to you? There's your Mercedes and dad's Mercedes, and I don't know who should get those cars or what should be done with them." When he heard about the "November to Remember" auction, he told her, "This is perfect. The cars will go to Mercedes people who will appreciate them like we do. It takes a lot of pressure off of both of us.'"

Even so, John Kraman, spokesman for industry giant Mecum Auctions, doubted sales like Mr. Baum's proposed generation-spanning transactions in Greenwich, Connecticut, would transform the Walworth, Wisconsin, firm's business anytime soon. "It's a fascinating concept," he said, "but a seller's biggest concern is and always will be, how much money can my car bring? Focusing on a single club-level event as opposed to a much wider audience makes me skeptical those expectations would be met." Some 30,000 cars a year cross Mecum's various U.S. auction blocks, he said; more than 3,000 vehicles change hands at its annual ten-day sale in Kissimmee, Florida, alone. "And telephone and internet bidding are already helping us attract buyers from a younger demographic."

That cold-eyed view wasn't shared by Mark Hyman, CEO and proprietor of Hyman Ltd., a prominent collectible car retailer in St. Louis, Missouri. "I think it's a fabulous idea," he said, "and I like the focus of it. The demographics of collecting have changed over the years. In the past, people collected old cars that were really toys to be driven on Sunday, not used for transportation. Now younger people buy '80s and '90s cars they can drive every day—to them, they're collector cars. Oftentimes, these same buyers—as they get older and wealthier—morph into the next generation of purchasers of truly rare collectibles."

Of course, in today's collector car world numerous platforms exist for dispatching with your vehicular treasure. However, most offer little contact between buyer and seller, generational or otherwise. The internet fairly

bristles with specialized auctions hoping to emulate the success of Bring-a-Trailer. Online sites like Craigslist, Autotrader, Car and Bids, and Bonhams, to mention just four, provide what are essentially virtual used car lots. Car shows, car club newsletters, and the old reliable sign in a window provide still more venues where the availability of a vehicle for sale may be made known.

Before you choose any of the above, however, the thoughtful seller is advised to thoroughly prepare their car for sale. Ed Adams, a Berkeley, California, resident who's independently bought and sold scores of collector cars over the years, offers a step-by-step guide to preparing for parting ways with your four-wheeled lover.

1. Get it looking as good as you possibly can. Give the car a "goodbye" hand washing and wax job yourself, or pay a professional detailer to do it for you. Touch up any paint chips. Get the engine steam-cleaned and maybe detailed

> Another presale rule: always get her looking as good as she can.

too. Clean and detail the interior. Use old toothbrushes and cotton swabs and spray-on products like Meguiar's Leather and Vinyl Cleaner. Besides cleaning and revitalizing plastic and vinyl surfaces, these products can prep leather for further protection. Vacuum under the seats and clear out the trunk. Hose off the undercarriage too; get it up on a lift or jacks and use a pressure nozzle.

2. Correct any outstanding mechanical problems. Hopefully you've been taking your car to a marque specialist. Consult with them *before* putting the vehicle up for sale. Make a to-do list. If the second gear synchros in your 1960s Alfa Romeo are worn—a not uncommon issue—fix 'em. If anything major can't be or hasn't been repaired, be sure to disclose those problems to the new owner.

3. Clean and box up any original parts. These should include factory-issued parts that were replaced and (if available) the owner's manual; original service and tire-changing tools; and any bags or storage gear that were part of the car's standard equipment when initially sold.

4. Be fully transparent about any and all cosmetic repairs and accidents or fender benders the car may have experienced. Mr. Adams recalls buying an apparently beautiful Mercedes 280 SL from a wealthy investment executive. On close examination it was revealed that the entire metal frame for the convertible top had gone missing, representing a $5,000 parts cost *before* replacing its cloth covering. Moreover, the Pagoda's "eyebrows," the iconic

> Before even thinking about selling, repair any and all body damage. Nobody's going to buy your bunged-up car (unless it's a Ferrari 250 GTO).

creases that run along the front fenders into matching notches in the headlight rims, had also disappeared. Their absence was a giveaway that the car had suffered front-end damage and been imperfectly repaired. The model in question was still a beauty, but its seller was forced to substantially reduce his price; Mr. Adams resold the car "as is" to an international broker in Holland.

5. Keep records, the more the better. Preserve the original build sheet if you have one. Compile an ownership history. Provide a file of all the work performed on the car during your ownership. Years ago, your author sold a car that had been damaged in a rear-end accident. The repair work was superb—the vehicle emerged in better shape than when it went in. But because all the costs were paid by the at-fault driver's insurance carrier, he failed to receive—and forgot to ask for—copies of the repair bills. It was his oversight, and

the car's subsequent buyer was justified in being chagrined by the omission. The lesson: every time a mechanic or body shop touches your vehicle—no matter how minor the task or service or whether a third party pays the bill— the work *must* be captured in a file that passes on to the next owner.

6. Decide on a price. Hagerty's Valuation Tool, Kelley Blue Book, Sports Car Market, and Classics.com are just a few sources for current values. Some of the sites offer a review of classic car sales by model over several years. Follow up on Bring-a-Trailer or other sites and decide where your year, model, and condition vehicle fits in. Professional assessors are also available, although most NextGen sellers can be guided by publicly available resources such as those suggested above.

7. Create and circulate a striking ad. Has your car won any awards—hint, the more the better. Even local club awards affirm your car's quality. What about rarity? Automakers like Ferrari, Lancia, Aston, and Alfa Romeo produced relatively miniscule numbers of models in the 1950s, '60s, and '70s, so make the most of

that low output. Was your car "coachbuilt," that is, mostly fashioned by hand by a body maker like Touring or Vignale? Was it painted an unusual color? At this writing, Mr. Adams was planning to sell his 1963 Porsche 356 coupe in Arctic White. Original rare colors have been known to add thousands of dollars to the selling price of vintage Porsches. Similarly, a four- or five-speed gearbox can bring important money to a vintage Mercedes SL; stick shift transmissions are almost always preferred over automatic ones even, in the case of some Ferraris and Maseratis, with early-edition paddle shifters.

8. Take it for a "farewell ride." As Nick Palermo advised on Autotrader.com a few years ago, "Plan one last hurrah on the open road. Make it big. Top off the tank, pack a lunch, and bring your favorite music."

9. Beware of scammers, especially if you sell your car online. A common ploy: the unseen "buyer" sends a cashier's check for more—often substantially more—than your car's asking price. The scammer then requests that you pay the difference to a nonexistent shipping company. The schemes work thanks to the widespread belief that cashier's checks are the same as cash. They're not and you may wind up literally holding an empty bag. You still have the car and you're out the "shipping" money.

10. Let go. Even if you sell your car to someone you meet in person and approve of, take comfort in knowing that it is going to a good home and move on. Don't "friend" its buyer on Facebook. "It's better not to be involved with a car once it is gone," advises Mr. Adams. "And never have regrets about selling a car."

Clean and box up ALL original parts; pass them on to the buyer.

One advantage in selling your vehicle at public auction, via firms such as Mecum, Bonhams, and Gooding & Co., is that, in most cases, you will already have signed over legal ownership to the auctioneer *before* "your" car crosses the block to its new owner.

"A car can become a significant emotional investment," sums up developmental psychologist and life coach Michelle R. Callahan in discussing the pangs felt by sellers. "It's there for major milestones, like weddings, babies, and graduations; it's literally the 'vehicle' that makes being physically present at these moments possible." A classic automobile can only deepen these feelings, as when a child or grandchild, for example, is hoisted behind the steering wheel at a car show. And for some, the entire parting-of-the-ways experience is avoided. As Jay Leno confessed to Classiccars.com, although he frequently donates automobiles to groups like the Wounded Warrior Project and Make-A-Wish Foundation, "I've never sold a car."

Hugo Modderman of Monaco pilots his 1930 Hispano Suiza H6C Cabriolet deVille through the Cascade Range during the Pebble Beach Motoring Classic from Washington State to Carmel, California.

12

THE ROAD AHEAD

"The Bailey Electric Roadster has startled the automobile world—
an electric that will average 20 miles per hour for 100 miles on one charge."
A Bailey Electric advertisement, circa 1910

"The designers of electric passenger car-carrying vehicles have made great advances in the past few years," the *New York Times* reported in 1911. A decade earlier, in 1889 and 1900 to be exact, electric-powered horseless carriages had outsold all other types of cars, according to Archive. Curbed.com. In all, nearly 2,000 electric automakers flourished and faded before finally sputtering out in the 1930s.

Today, what was old seems new again.

THEN: Riker Electric owned by the same Oregon family since it was purchased new in 1896.

THE OTTISES AND THE TRENERYS: A GENERATIONAL COMMENTARY

Are the same factors at play now as those at the beginning of the last century, albeit for more globally significant reasons? Will most of us be driving electric cars in the future? We think they are, and we will. Will electric vehicles once again return as the dominant form of transportation? Again, it appears so. Will our conversion to electric transport happen as quickly and smoothly as its advocates, government bureaucrats, and loathers of petrol think, hope, and want? Most likely not—only time will tell.

But assuming the world does eventually plunge fully and successfully into the electric car age, will that mark the demise of vintage collectible cars as automotive dinosaurs? As fossils, if you will, of the Fossil Fuel Age?

Patrick Ottis and his NextGen son Tazio, of Patrick Ottis Co., in Berkeley, California, don't think so. And neither do Bruce Trenery and his NextGen son Spencer, of Fantasy Junction, in nearby Emeryville, California. But just how do they assess the future of collectible cars? In

WHEN: Audi Shark Concept Flying Sports Car.

late 2021 interviews, we sought the opinions of these generation-spanning father-and-son teams because as a foursome and for decades—in the process of building separate but equal international reputations—they've collectively devoted their entire professional lives to buying, selling, preserving, and restoring some of the world's rarest and most beautiful automobiles. And, perhaps most to the point, their respective livelihoods depend on continuing to do so.

Father-Son Team One: Ferrari Restorers Patrick and Tazio Ottis: "We're very busy right now, and we've got a waiting list. I can't see that slowing down any time soon."

PATRICK OTTIS, 71

Born and raised in Oklahoma, Mr. Ottis boasts a resumé that would arouse envy and respect in any motoring enthusiast. As a teenager, he revived a 1935 Ford five-window coupe he'd purchased for $50. After college studies in mechanical engineering, Mr. Ottis joined notable Ferrari restorer and repairer Alf Francis, then based in Wichita, Kansas. Mr. Francis had previously worked throughout Europe as lead mechanic for Stirling Moss and the Rob Walker Racing Team.

After six years with Alf Francis, Mr. Ottis moved to California, where he worked for another well-known incubator of talent, Stephen Griswold. Son of the winner of the first U.S. Grand Prix, Mr. Griswold had an attention to detail that made him a legend among vintage auto enthusiasts; based in Northern California, he sold, serviced, repaired, and reconditioned Ferraris, Alfa Romeos, Maseratis, and Aston Martins. He would often disassemble a vehicle and strip its body in an acid tank. Every nut and bolt from every car was cleaned and washed and returned to its original condition. "Griswold Restorations was a talented group," Mr. Ottis recalls. "The machinists were the best in the world, the panel beaters were the best in the world, and the mechanics were the best in the world." All told, the firm won seven Best Ferrari and Best Race Car awards at Pebble Beach Concours d'Elegance.

When Mr. Griswold moved to Europe in the early 1980s, his gifted alumni—Mr. Ottis among them—scattered around Berkeley's flatlands, hanging out their own shingles. Many went on to build impressive reputations. Of Mr. Ottis, declared *Car and Driver* in 2012, "If it is true that there are no more than a dozen people in the U.S. capable of constructing a superlative vintage Ferrari V-12 engine, then Patrick Ottis is, in most experts' views, among the very best." Besides winning and helping many others win trophies for Alfa Romeo, Maserati, and Ferrari cars, Mr. Ottis serves on the International Advisory Council for the Preservation of the Ferrari Automobile, and regularly scours the globe in search of restoration parts for clients as far away as London and Bahrain. Indeed, in 2018, not long after a Ferrari 250 GTO achieved $48.4 million to become the most expensive automobile ever publicly sold, its engine stood on a repair stand in Mr. Ottis's shop.

WHAT'S AHEAD

PATRICK: "Electric is the future for sure, but in May 2022, for me, it will be fifty years of repairing Ferrari automobiles—all with an internal combustion engine. Over the years I've become a student of—and fascinated by—the practical engineers who developed and built the cars that we work on here," he says. "Vittorio Jano, Harry Miller, Giacomo Colombo. We've made a study of how all these wonderful engines developed. A driver I'm not, but as a practical engineer I'm a student and a fan of where all of this came from. There's still enough interest in historic cars that that's how it's going to play out for me."

TAZIO OTTIS, 26

"It really is like I've been here all my life," says Tazio Ottis. "Before I could drive in high school, it was just a skateboard ride down to the shop." By the age of thirteen, the younger Mr. Ottis was full-bore into kart racing and, when he turned fifteen and a half, the aforementioned Trenerys sponsored him in SCCA driver's training in one of their Miatas.

Along the way and before formally joining Patrick Ottis Co., Tazio interned with Jim Groom, another highly regarded Griswold alumni, who specialized in servicing vintage Jaguar sports and racing cars.

Passionate about open-wheel cars since his childhood, Tazio began racing Formula One Mazdas, winning a string of checkered flags at nearby Sears Point and other tracks. He soon came under the wing of Mazda stars Eric Purcell, an MIT-trained engineer and A-list F1 driver in the United States and Europe, and champion open-wheeler and driver-coach Chuck West. In late 2021, Tazio partnered with Chinese film actor and race car enthusiast Daniel Wu to take a big next step: formation of their own team racing formula Honda Civics.

MARKETPLACE TRENDS

TAZIO: "Ferraris from the late '80s and '90s have almost tripled in value in the last five years. There's obviously still huge interest in the Ferrari brand and they're still heavily invested in all forms of motorsports. They're reentering Le Mans; they're building a new chassis that will most likely be hybrid powered."

PATRICK: "We've just taken on a talented mechanic with forty years of Ferrari experience. He's totally conversant with all the new Ferraris, including La Ferrari. Since he's been here I've driven a couple of the newer mid-engine 488s; you get out of a 1965 and then you get in a three- or four-year-old Ferrari and it's unbelievable; it's just so great—I can't even appreciate it. Young guys like Tazio can really use a car like that. And that's when I recognize how amazing the future is. And that it's just going to continue."

TAZIO: "I'm not afraid of an autopilot car. Driving down the I-5 can be tedious, especially when you do it once or twice every two or three weeks. So if a car had an autonomous mode and I could sit back and relax, check my email and so on, I wouldn't be opposed to that. Some of the modern supercars are like a 1969–1974 Dino—nice to drive to a coffee shop. They are easy around town because they are light to steer. There's a joy in that to me."

Peering into the future of the Patrick Ottis Co., one could begin to understand how and why two Ottis generations could seem so similarly confident—despite their separation by nearly fifty years. On their near-term shop calendar were high-end rebuilding jobs starring an ultra rare Ferrari GT Zagato and a Tour de France Berlinetta, the latter in need of a complete nuts-and-bolts restoration prior to being shown nationally. And looming in the recent rearview mirror: a just-finished 250 GTO for a client in New York and yet another class win at Pebble Beach. Best of all, after resolving some balky piston issues, there would be more track time for Tazio in the shop's very own Scaglietti-sculpted Ferrari 750 Monza Spyder (see chapter 10, "Finding Your Tribe"). "That can always be ours," said Tazio. He nodded toward the gleaming white sports car. "As long as we can get race gas."

THE FUTURE
PATRICK: "Tazio has already taken the first steps here. He's become involved in the banking and parts sourcing and administrative end of our business. He's good at it and I'm not. So I think that's going to be the path. We just attended a vintage weekend at Laguna Seca, where there was wild enthusiasm for the historic racing class. There's still enough money and passion for us to make a business out of it. We are very busy right now and we've got a waiting list. I can't see that slowing down anytime soon."

BRUCE TRENERY, 73

"I became interested in sports cars when I was about ten years old," says Bruce Trenery, founder of Fantasy Junction, the globally successful purveyor of collectible cars based in Emeryville, California. "A friend of mine had a sports car book—we would spend hours going through each chapter, Mercedes 300 SLs, 120 Jags, Ferrari 250 GTs, etc." In high school and college Mr. Trenery raced open-wheel Formula C and Vee cars in Sports Car Club of America events. "I was never interested in being a new car dealer," the Berkeley native recalls, but as an international marketing major at nearby San Francisco State College, "I got the idea that maybe you could make a living having an exotic car store."

After acquiring the company name from a Marin County BMW dealer for $500, Mr. Trenery opened Fantasy Junction's doors in Berkeley in 1976. Thirteen years later, he moved the firm to larger quarters in nearby Emeryville. In addition to its capacious brick-walled showroom, the new location's neighborhood was steeped in automotive history—with former outposts of both the Fisher Body and Doble Steam Motors companies were located nearby.

Today, Fantasy Junction serves an international clientele; Mr. Trenery travels the world in search of interesting automobiles. Still maintaining a keen interest in motorsports, he's participated in both the Daytona 24-hour and Nurbürgring 24-hour events and Laguna Seca's Monterey Historics, along with modern amateur

racing and many rallies. "Whether pounding down the Mulsanne straight at Le Mans in a Delahaye or a Ferrari," declared a company write up, "Bruce enjoys the competition to the fullest."

SPENCER TRENERY, 42

"I first came here in diapers and on Saturdays played on the floor with Hot Wheels and Legos," says Spencer Trenery. His eyes drift across rows of collectible vehicles. "I grew up with all these cars around me."

Following in his father's footsteps—and anticipating those of Tazio Ottis—the younger Mr. Trenery raced karts at age nine and then moved up and on. At seventeen, he became the youngest ever Sports Car Club of America Pro Racing champion. In 2018, he captured the national GT2 championship in SCCA closed-wheel sports car racing.

CHANGING DEMOGRAPHICS

BRUCE: "The collectors are younger. Generally, buyers choose cars they wanted when they were young. So with the buyer who now is fifty years old, you go back thirty years and you are in the 1970s or later. There are exceptions. Bentley collectors are still extremely active, so 1928 to the early 1930s models are extremely popular. The collector interest in supercharged Alfas from that era is still super strong and very well heeled. Those are late '20s and '30s cars that people still want and probably always will. Likewise Bugattis of the same period."

CHANGING CARS

BRUCE: "The cars that aren't likely to do well are more practical, mass-produced cars. Closed cars. Those cars usually don't financially justify the restoration costs. Some of them are architecturally beautiful, but they're not something people would use on a rally. The cars that can be used on a rally—the California or Italian Mille—those will be popular, but only for sports cars. So you could have a Mercedes 300 SL and have a lot of fun, but if you have a handbuilt Adenauer 300 [1957–1962] sedan, nobody's going to muscle it around two-lane roads. And if you restore those two cars, the sedan will probably be more because there's more paint, more interior work, and the mechanical stuff is roughly the same. The value of the sports car will normally be much higher."

NEW VENUES

BRUCE: "Compared to twenty-five years ago, there are many more 1,000-mile casual rallies than ever before. There are more vintage race groups, more track events—track days—where people can go out and drive out on a track with a car that's not really a race-prepared car. They drive them more gently. Examples would include modern R-Type Mustangs, Lotus Elises, a 360 Challenge Ferrari, or a Porsche Cup car, for people who don't want the stress of full competition. There's Green Flag ["where fans become drivers"] events. All these happenings are becoming more popular."

SPENCER: "This last weekend at the Velocity Invitational at Laguna Seca they had eight historic racing events each day. In between them the modern McLaren group were lapping their 620s and 740s or whatever; people could sign up and go for a ride with a professional driver in a modern McLaren. The McLaren people could also stand next to a McLaren Speedtail [fastest McLaren ever, top speed of 250 mph, only twenty-eight in the world] that was on display. So there's a whole culture around that one type of car."

WHICH CARS ARE LIKELY TO INCREASE IN VALUE?

BRUCE: "Beautiful and sexy cars, a Ferrari 275/4, a California Spyder, or Mercedes Gullwing— those cars are art and they still have a chance to grow. But it's going to be harder. Cities like London don't really want you driving around in an old car, and younger buyers don't want to go out in today's traffic in something that's likely to have problems."

THE CULTURE OF COLLECTIBLE CARS

SPENCER: "The cars here at Fantasy Junction have little in common with ordinary cars. And that insulates them and us from a business perspective from some of the problems that you might think we'd confront.

"People don't use the cars we sell as cars, as a transportation utility. But they love the social interaction surrounding them. So there's a culture around each car. If you're into Porsches, there's a Porsche Cars and Coffee, there's a Porsche Meet and Greet, and there's Porsche Luftgekühlt [huge, air-cooled rallies]. If you're a Lamborghini person, there's a once-annual Miura tour. There's a culture around historic competition.

Whatever type of car you're interested in, there's a culture surrounding that car for you to join and be part of. So there are all these cultural pockets and people really ground themselves and identify with other people based on the pocket they're in.

"And that's why the cars we sell don't need to be utilitarian. Their use is structured around specific experiential purposes—the California Mille; racing at Laguna Seca; showing a car at Quail Lodge. They've risen above the necessity of being relied upon as a traditional automobile.

"Take the annual London to Brighton run. These cars are unbelievably irrelevant as motor cars. But on social media I see where young twenty- and thirty-somethings are in awe of the fact that they still exist at all and how different they are from what they consider to be an automobile. Yet for eight hours a year, the cars have a specific purpose and it's very prestigious to participate and people think it's the coolest thing under the sun. And that's really breathed a huge breath of life into very early and pre-1900s cars."

VIRTUAL RELATIONSHIPS

BRUCE: "Another thing is the accessibility of everything on the internet. If you had an Alfa Romeo 2600 in 1980 and you needed a grill or a left front fender it could be really hard to find one. Now you can go to the Alfa bulletin board on the web and somebody will say, 'I've got one.' You can find things that without the internet you couldn't find for years and years. And that makes a car that's very rare still viable because you can actually get parts for it."

SPENCER: "Over the years, I've had a number of transactions with a supremely knowledgeable gentleman. But in the dozen or so times I've sold cars to him—and sometimes for him—I've never met him in person and he's never been to this continent. He's never touched one of the cars. These are cars that are nearing $10 million. At times we've kept his cars in storage, and resold them again, and been deeply involved in their restorations. We've shown them at Pebble Beach. So you think, 'How does he extract enjoyment out of this?' Yet he really knows about the cars. For example, when we're restoring a car, he'll say, 'We shouldn't make this or that compromise; let's spend the money to get it right.' So he's very emotionally involved, but not in physically operating the cars at all. Or even touching them."

INFLATION HEDGE

SPENCER: "Competitively and economically, the collectible car is freer from the challenges of modernization than you might expect. And if there really is a significant inflationary period, they may well benefit. Because a collectible car is a physical asset that can be moved from one place to another. In terms of rare and valuable things, it's diversified from real estate in that way. So that could be a benefit if inflationary forces stay with us."

BRUCE: "The stock market has been going up for ten years—people ask, 'Is this going to go on forever?' And if the government keeps spending, we're likely to see prolonged inflation. So if you're worried about the stock market, worried about inflation, then having hard assets like these cars probably makes some financial sense. If the economies are stronger in Europe or Japan, the cars can go to Europe or Japan. Whereas if you own a condo in downtown Oakland or San Francisco, you can't move it someplace else."

URBAN FLIGHT

SPENCER: "I think the next ten years will involve a decentralization of the car culture outside of dense urban areas. I see it in London now. Young dealers are buying small farms and repurposing them in the Cotswolds and other rural areas where they can have a small showroom and offices. They don't want to be or can't be in downtown London—they can't afford it; the regulations discourage it; parking is a drag. Ten years ago, the view was that if you wanted to be successful in a business of affluence you needed to be in the densest urban centers. But urban centers have become less appealing, certainly in the last twenty-four months than they were, for reasons that don't necessarily have to do with cars but accidentally seem to benefit cars. There's an uncomfortable economic stratification happening in urban environments.

"So it seems there's a quickly growing audience of people operating their cars outside of urban centers, and that's going to be a trend going forward. If you want to own and drive an interesting car, it's a lot more pleasant to do it out of Sonoma County than it is to leave out of your storage building in Oakland, Berkeley, or San Francisco."

BRUCE: "Autonomous cars, where you get in the car and go back to doing what you're doing on your tablet or phone, are going to be more popular, especially with younger people, because they can get more work done while in traffic. If you had a choice of driving your 120 Jag that's going to overheat in bridge traffic on your way to San Francisco or sitting in an autonomous car and talking to your partner or maybe doing a couple of emails, which one would you choose—even if you're a car person?"

SPENCER: "When there's an autonomous car that's broadly manufactured and broadly used and trouble free, I'll have two of 'em. As quickly as they are available and I can afford it."

AUTONOMOUS CARS

For the moment, of course, autonomous cars, let alone self-driving *enthusiast* cars, remain an approaching if not a distant reality. "If you look at where modern cars are going, I definitely think autonomous operation will become part of the future enthusiast car experience," Chris Gerdes, codirector of Stanford University's Center for Automotive Research, told your author in a 2022 *New York Times* interview. "It will be very possible to build cars that enthusiasts love to drive when they want to and then can switch to autonomous operation when they don't."

Even so, creating and orchestrating the complex mosaic of automated cameras and sensors, machine-learning tools, and algorithms needed to achieve safe and reliable self-driving cars is no small challenge. "A successful autonomous system requires that the self-driving vehicle be constantly aware of other objects and conveyances," Mr. Gerdes noted. That includes automobiles, trucks, buses, bicycles, pedestrians, and "how traffic moves down a street or highway, where other vehicles are in relation to the autonomous car—and then it must be able to execute any and all necessary corrective actions, including stopping."

By late 2021, the National Highway Traffic Safety Administration had reported at least a dozen accidents involving Tesla cars operating on autopilot, three of them fatal. A California Tesla driver became the first motorist charged with a felony in an autopilot accident that claimed two lives. And that same year, a driverless start-up based in Silicon Valley and Guangzhou, China, lost its state testing permit when its vehicle crashed in Fremont, California.

CNN's Matt McFarland reported needing "plenty of human intervention" when putting Tesla's Full Self-Driving Mode through its paces. "Numerous times," he said, the network's human driver had to physically intervene to avoid a crash. And even if such technology were flawless, automated cars face steep psychological hurdles. Unlike passive air travel, where highly trained commercial pilots have a personal stake in keeping you—and themselves—alive, "riding in a fully autonomous car means putting our faith in hardware and algorithms," wrote James Meigs in *Commentary*.

Tesla vehicles faced other problems as well. The J. D. Power Initial Quality Study in 2021 found Tesla's Model 3 vehicles fell below average in their range. Equally troubling, a separate report comparing that same model to its year newer version (2022) suggested build quality had deteriorated even further. The Finnish owner of a used Model S ($80,000 to $120,000 new, depending on options) became so frustrated with his car's problems and Tesla's allegedly lackluster response that he taped explosives to the vehicle and blew it up. A mannequin wearing an Elon Musk mask was strapped into the driver's seat.

Electric vehicles (EVs) faced other obstacles as well. The continued availability of titanium cobalt, lithium, nickel, and other rare materials needed in batteries is one. The ability of utility power grids to reliably supply the needs of an all-electric society is another.

Besides such tangible shortcomings, there were more subjective, more intangible qualities that could prolong the life of internal combustion engine (ICE) cars, most specifically, *collectible* ICE cars. It is a barrier that, to achieve ultimate success, EVs and, in fact, most modern cars, must overcome. In a word, are today's cars—fossil-fuel-free or not—*beautiful* enough? Or, to state it more unkindly, are they beautiful at all? And if they're not, can they ever hope to fully achieve collectability?

After attending the Los Angeles Auto Show, *New York Times* opinion essayist Farhad Manjoo described the experience as "as bland and monotonous as a supermarket's TV dinner aisle." His 2021 article went on to state, "Cars may be undergoing huge changes on the inside, but you wouldn't know it to look at them. Cars were once a playground for aesthetic experimentation, a showcase for the world's most inventive and daring industrial designers. Now they really are like smartphones; every new iPhone is only a slight evolution from the last one, and so is every new car. Every year the product side of cars offers less to love." While lauding automotive advances in electronics, computers, and artificial intelligence, Mr. Manjoo concluded with a lament: "I just wish they weren't also losing heart, soul, and personality."

But what if electricity could make old cars new again? Could the road ahead include a possible path to preserving the beauty of vintage vehicles in a future all-EV world? In a *New York Times* article titled "Vintage Cars with Electric-Heart Transplants," your author reported on initiatives by both Aston Martin and Jaguar to replace petrol-burning engines with electric power trains in classic models. Indeed, the piece recounted how Prince Harry and Meghan Markle silently motored off from their 2018 wedding in a kilowatt-powered E-type Jaguar.

"We want to give our heritage cars greater longevity," explained Paul Spires, president of Aston Martin Works. "We'd hate for them all to just wind up gathering dust in museums, where no one can actually enjoy a classic Aston on the road."

As with Jaguar's "Concept Zero" E-Type, the only external clue to the true power source in Aston's converted 1970 DB6 was the glowing digital screen nestled in its dashboard. Perhaps most surprising, a *Car and Driver* test drive of the Jag concluded it handled well and never felt short of traction. "Battery Power Doesn't Ruin the Jaguar E-Type," read *Car and Driver*'s headline.

Even Martin Button, a member of the Pebble Beach Concours d'Elegance selection team, saw a potential upside in electrified classic automobiles. In fact, he suggested, such conversions might "inoculate" older vehicles such as Duesenbergs, Packards, and Delahayes against ever-tightening air-quality regulations. Of course, for show purposes, the original engines would need to be reinstalled, a task the British automakers estimated would take about a week's shop time.

Consider the opportunities such modifications might offer. Many of history's most compelling automotive designs were sketched and sculpted decades ago, often during the 1930s, an era historians often describe as a golden age of creativity—in films (*Gone with the Wind*, *Stagecoach*, *Ninotchka*), literature (Ernest Hemingway, F. Scott Fitzgerald, Erich Maria Remarque), music (Benny Goodman, Bing Crosby, Fred Astaire), and art (Grant Wood, Pablo Picasso, Georgia O'Keeffe), to cite just a few. Now picture yourself cruising up Italy's Amalfi Coast or past the giant redwoods that fringe California's rugged northern shoreline. Gliding silently beside you might be one of the beauties pictured in the gallery on the following pages.

Above: 1930 Ruxton Model C Roadster by Baker-Raulang. America's first front-wheel drive, *Automobile Quarterly* described the Ruxton as "A superb automobile that never had a chance." Although its April 1929 announcement as America's first front-drive passenger car preceded Cord's, the marque's lifetime lasted just 20 months and produced only 96 cars. Nonetheless, the Ruxton's advanced technology and stylish looks have led experts to include the ill-fated car among the elite vehicles of its era.

Below: Left to right: a 1937 Hispano Suiza Chapron-bodied K-6 coach; 1934 Packard 1100 Sedan; 1932 Lincoln KB Roadster pause during the Pebble Beach Motoring Classic. Many Motoring Classic participants have previously been shown at the Pebble Beach Concours d'Elegance.

Above: 1937 Delage D8 120. Typically fitted with bespoke bodies by Paris coachbuilders, Delage cars were among the most advanced offerings by French automakers. The D8 120 Aerosport Coupe, for example, preceded the first American pillarless hardtops by a full ten years.

Below: 1939 Alfa Romeo 2900 Coupe. Considered among the most stylish cars of their era, the Touring-bodied 2900 Berlinettas featured fully-independent suspension and eight-cyclinder supercharged engines designed by the legendary Victor Jano.

Above: 1934 Hispano Suiza J 12 Fernandez and Darrin Coupe de Ville. The ultraluxurious J12 Hispanos competed head-to-head with Alfa, Bugatti, and other contemporary marques thanks to their 5-foot-long, 10-liter V-12 power plants. Among the priciest pre-war chassis, the J-12 was engineered for near-silent operation.

Below: 1939 Alfa Romeo 6C 2500 SS Berlinetta Aerodinamica. Writing in *Sports Car Market*, collector Miles Collier called this Touring-bodied Alfa "the pinnacle of pre-war Italian design, combining the best of elegance, aerodynamics, and competitive purpose." Despite no surviving originals, those qualities are readily apparent in this exacting re-creation by noted restorers Dino Cognolato and Nino Epifani on an authentic pre-war 2500 SS chassis.

Above: 1947 Talbot Lago T-26 GS Coupe. Winner of the 24 hours of Le Mans in 1950, the rare and exquisite T-26 was one of its era's fastest luxury cars. Only 30 of the GS models were built, each fitted with a high-performance 4.5-liter six-cylinder engine and capable of reaching 125 miles per hour. Along with high-end French marques like Bugatti, Delage, and Delahaye, Talbot-Lago struggled financially after World War II before finally folding in 1959.

Below: 1938 Alfa Touring 2900B Corto Spider. Surely among the most beautiful open cars ever designed, Alfa's curvaceous 140-mile-per-hour short wheelbase 2900B debuted as the world's fastest production car. First- and second-place finishers in the 1938 Mille Miglia, the 2900B won the race again in 1947. The slatted rear skirts were removable for accessing the wheels.

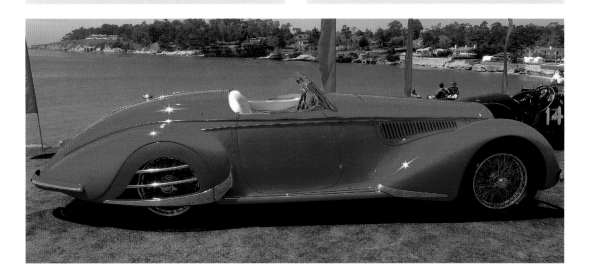

In a 2022 interview with the *New York Times*, Randy Nonnenberg, president and founder of Bring-a-Trailer.com, spoke with your author about the importance of visual appeal to future collector car sales and, for that matter, to today's fossil-powered automobiles and EVs as well.

"It's still eye-opening design elements that make cars interesting," Mr. Nonnenberg observed. "The more today's designs become jelly-bean-like, the more prized the older cars that go through Bring-a-Trailer will become. Many of the true vintage cars really are pieces of art. They're lovely to look at and they make a real impact."

Despite the pandemic—or partly because of it—collector car sales enjoyed a roaring, soaring year in 2021. BaT's gross results approached the $900 million mark, making it the world's largest single marketplace for the sale of collectible vehicles. That stellar performance continued into 2022. Meanwhile, tentpole auctioneer Mecum opened with a $217 million take at its annual eleven-day, Kissimmee, Florida, sale in January 2022. It was the highest figure ever for a single live car auction. On Saturday, January 15, Mecum recorded $72

QUIET BEAUTY
UK-based Hemmels converts classic sports cars to silent-running kilowatt power. The firm's specialty: retrofitting Mercedes' iconic Pagoda sports cars like this 280 SL. The firm sources its own donor cars for bespoke buyers, and, after full restoration, installs a battery pack, AC motor, and regenerative braking. The "new" 280 delivers about 180 horsepower and a 170-mile range. Price: $325,000.

million for that day alone; overall, the event saw more than 3,000 vehicles pass under the hammer at a 90 percent sell-through rate.

Aesthetics may have played a part in those numbers, but deeper human motives were important too. After two years of lockdowns, mask mandates, and vaccinations, "people needed an escape," said Mr. Nonnenberg. "Folks seemed to have a dream of getting out into the country, away from the confined spaces that COVID had imposed on us. Even if they were in an urban area, they wanted to have a foothold in that dream." Those emotions were almost certainly reflected in BaT's sharply increased demand for classic trucks and four-wheel drives—Scouts, Broncos, Blazers, Land Cruisers, and old farm pickup trucks.

COVID drove more people to the internet and made them increasingly comfortable with shopping, buying, and selling online, Mr. Nonnenberg continued. "A lot of them came to our site"—Bring-a-Trailer logged more than 300,000 new users during the pandemic—"and there were also a lot of people relocating their lives. I really think those two are tied together." He called it "a freedom narrative."

Does that thirst for freedom exclude the screens and buzzers and government-mandated gadgets that allegedly protect us? Is it because of that thirst that we turn away from designs that have lost their heart, soul, and personality? Is there something inherently liberating in even a 1990s car that is free of them? Your author drives a Series 1 Lexus SC 300 coupe. After 250,000 miles and twenty-five years, its original

paint still sparkles, its black-on-black leather interior remains cosseting, its six cylinders deliver as-new compression, and its refreshed suspension bends corners with aplomb.

Even if they are less practical for daily use, we somehow find our feelings of freedom enhanced as we drift back in time to consider still older automobiles, to the flowing, uninhibited curves of their "raindrop" fender lines; to the full-throated howl of their thrusting, pounding pistons; to the firm, reassuring feedback of their unpowered steering.

Why do we flock to events featuring century-old automobiles on bumpy journeys between ancient cities on Britain's foggy coast? Why do we attend races of historic—and historically slow—cars in California? Why do we rent garages out of town to house fifty-year-old vehicles? Is it because, as Ralph Fiennes's Basil Brown declares in *The Dig*, that "the past speaks"? Or is it because we need to prove to ourselves that we are, in fact, still free? Or, perhaps, because both are true?

The road ahead may be riddled with potholes, but it is also a pathway to memories that remind us of who we are and what we hope to be. And somehow, for growing numbers of us, that road is enhanced when it is traveled in a beautiful, comfy, doo-daddle-free, old car.

Taking Aim at the Future: 1931–38 Pierce Arrow "Unhelmeted Archer" hood ornament.

RESOURCES

AMERICA'S AUTOMOTIVE TRUST (AAT)
www.americasautomotivetrust.org
2702 East D St.
Tacoma, WA 98421
253-779-8490

THE HAGERTY DRIVERS FOUNDATION
(Incorporating the Heritage Vehicle Association)
Corporate.hagerty.com/driversfoundation
P.O. Box 1303
Traverse City, MI 49685-1303
877-922-9701

MCPHERSON COLLEGE
www.mcpherson.edu
1600 E. Euclid St.
McPherson, Kansas 67460
800-365-7402

THE PEBBLE BEACH COMPANY FOUNDATION
www.pebblebeach.com/pbc-foundation
P.O. Box 1767
Pebble Beach, CA 93953
831-649-7651

THE PETERSEN AUTOMOTIVE MUSEUM
www.petersen.org/business-incubator-program
6060 Wilshire Blvd.
Los Angeles, CA 90036
323-930-2277

RPM FOUNDATION
https://rpm.foundation
2702 East D. St.
Tacoma, WA 98421
855-537-4579

SAN FRANCISCO ACADEMY OF ART
www.academyart.edu
79 New Montgomery St.
San Francisco, CA 94105
800-544-2787

SHIFTING GEARS
gsevents.live/contact
Cindy Sisson
cindy@gsevents.live
704-906-9507

STANFORD UNIVERSITY CENTER FOR AUTOMOTIVE RESEARCH
https://cars.stanford.edu
416 Escondido Mall, MC 4021
Stanford, CA 94305-2203
650-736-4322

TECHFORCE FOUNDATION
https://techforce.org
4848 E. Cactus Rd. #505-304
Scottsdale, AZ 85254
866-519-6923

ABOUT THE AUTHOR

Robert C. Yeager's love for cars began as a 16-year-old high schooler when he purchased a "raked," baby-blue 1940 Ford two-door coupe for $250. Other cars of his youth included a 1948 Cadillac 7-passenger sedan and, in college, a red 1957 Studebaker Silver Hawk. As an adult, Yeager has owned a series of award-winning vintage Alfa Romeos. His current "fun" cars include an all-original 1972 Mercedes Benz 450 SL—recently awarded a Silver Star Preservation Award by the Mercedes Benz Club of America—and a 1996 Lexus SC 300.

For the past decade-plus, Yeager has written about collectible cars for the *New York Times*. Other previously published credits include *Readers Digest*; *Family Circle*; *Woman's Day*; *Encyclopedia Britannica*; and others. His byline has also appeared in the *Chicago Tribune*, *New Orleans Times-Picayune*, and the *New York Times Service*.

In 2013, Yeager's novel, *The Romanov Stone*, won an Independent Publisher's "Ippy" for suspense/thrillers, and an IndieReader Discovery Award for General Fiction.

Yeager resides in Oakland and at The Sea Ranch, both in California.

IMAGE CREDITS

L = Left; R = Right; T = Top; B = Bottom

ALAMY: 15, 24, 36, 39, 40, 41, 46, 54L, 57R, 70, 71, 72, 74, 76, 87, 114, 173B

ARCHIVIO MARIANI, ITALY: 66

BRINGATRAILER.COM: 18, 127, 146-147

BRITISH MUSEUM: 14

BRUCE MEYER: 80

CAITLIN O'HARA: 140-141

CREATIVE COMMONS: 75, 84, 94, 122-123

GETTY: 53, 67, 90, 92

HAGERTY: 4, 8, 9, 10, 11, 12-13, 20, 23, 33, 34, 38, 57L, 60, 61, 62, 64, 69, 77, 82, 88, 91, 96, 98, 101, 106-107, 108, 109, 112, 116, 119, 120, 121, 125, 126, 129, 130, 131, 133, 134, 135, 136, 138, 148, 149, 150, 151, 152, 160, 162, 163, 168, 169, 170, 171

HEMMELS: 186

KIMBALL STOCK: 30, 95

LAURA FOSTER: 142

LIBRARY OF CONGRESS, PRINTS & PHOTOGRAPHS DIVISION: 26

MAGIC CAR: 43, 54R, 55, 56, 58, 63

MICHAEL FURMAN AND THE MULLIN AUTOMOTIVE MUSEUM: 29

MPACREATIVE: 21, 22

RENEE BRINKERHOFF/VALKYRIE RACING: 143

ROBERT YEAGER: 16, 19, 27, 28, 31, 44, 51, 59, 78, 79, 113, 153, 154-155, 156, 157, 158, 159, 161, 164, 165, 172, 173T, 174, 177, 182, 183, 184, 185, 187

RON POLLARD: 139

ROXIE HENDRY: 166

SHUTTERSTOCK: 25, 42, 52, 85, 99, 102-103, 104, 111, 117

THE W. EDWARDS DEMING INSTITUTE: 47

ZACK MILLER COLLECTION: 32

INDEX